STUDIES IN ANTHROPOLOGICAL METHOD

General Editors

GEORGE AND LOUISE SPINDLER
Stanford University

UNDERSTANDING AN AFRICAN KINGDOM: BUNYORO

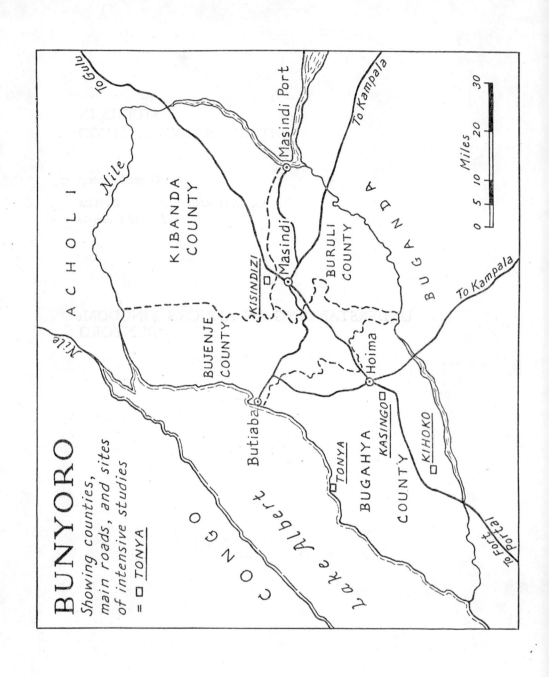

BUNYORO

Showing counties,
main roads, and sites
of intensive studies

= □ *TONYA*

KIBANDA COUNTY

BURULI COUNTY

BUJENJE COUNTY

BUGAHYA COUNTY

KISINDIZI

Masindi

TONYA

KASINGO

KIHOKO

Masindi Port

Hoima

Butiaba

ACHOLI

BUGANDA

CONGO

Lake Albert

Nile

N.ile

To Gulu

To Kampala

To Kampala

To Fort Portal

Miles

0   5   10   20   30

UNDERSTANDING AN
AFRICAN KINGDOM:
BUNYORO

JOHN BEATTIE
Oxford University

HOLT, RINEHART AND WINSTON
New York   Chicago   San Francisco   Toronto   London

To

E.-P.

FOREWORD

About the Series

Anthropology has been, since the turn of the century, a significant influence shaping Western thought. It has brought into proper perspective the position of our culture as one of many, and has challenged universalistic and absolutistic assumptions and beliefs about the proper condition of man. Anthropology, the study of man, has been able to make this contribution mainly through its descriptive analyses of unfamiliar ways of life. Only in the last decades of anthropology's comparatively short existence as a science have anthropologists developed systematic theories about human behavior in its transcultural dimensions. Only still more recently have anthropological techniques of data collection and analysis become explicit.

Nearly every issue of every professional anthropological journal contains statements of methodological innovations. Our discipline is in a seminal period of development.

Teachers of anthropology have previously been handicapped by the lack of clear, authoritative statements of how anthropologists collect and analyze relevant data. The results of fieldwork are available in the ethnographers' published works. Although these demonstrate cultural diversity and integration, social control, religious behavior, marriage customs, and the like, they rarely tell students much about how the facts have been gathered and interpreted. Without this information the alert "consumer" of anthropological results is left uninformed about the processes of our science—an unsatisfying state of affairs for both the student and the professor.

Our Studies in Anthropological Method series is designed to help fill this gap. Each study in the series focuses upon some manageable aspect of modern anthropological methodology. Each one demonstrates significant aspects of the processes of gathering, ordering, and interpreting data. Some are highly selected dimensions of methodology. Others are concerned with the whole range of experience involved in studying a total society. The studies are written by professional anthropologists who have done fieldwork and have made significant contributions to the science of man and his works. The authors explain how they go about this work, and to what end. We believe the studies will be helpful to students—in courses ranging from the introductory to the graduate level—who want to know what processes of inquiry and ordering stand behind the formal, published results of anthropology.

About the Author

John Beattie, the author of the case study *Bunyoro: An African Kingdom,* is a Senior Lecturer in Social Anthropology at Oxford University, where is he a Fellow of Linacre College. His first degree was in philosophy, and he spent eight years in Tanganyika (now Tanzania) during the 1940s as an administrative officer. He was a Fellow of the Center for Advanced Study in the Behavioral Sciences at Stanford, California, during 1959–1960. He is the author of *Other Cultures* (1964), and has published articles on aspects of social anthropology as well as on Nyoro social and cultural institutions.

About the Book

This is the story of the fieldwork that stands behind *Bunyoro: An African Kingdom* by John Beattie in the Case Studies in Cultural Anthropology series. Making contacts with officials, choosing a field site, setting up a household, explaining one's role, giving and attending beer parties and other social affairs, visiting homes and being visited, learning the language—all of these activities that make up anthropological fieldwork and that give specific meaning to the term "participant observation" are described in detail. Dr. Beattie also informs the reader about the more formal techniques of data collection he employed, such as conducting interviews, collecting case histories, using official records, constructing and using questionnaires, carrying out a house to house survey, and a most ingenious use of an essay competition. A conception of what an anthropologist actually does in the field emerges that is almost totally lacking in conventional ethnographies, or for that matter in the whole published anthropological literature. Though no two anthropologists go about their work in quite the same way and no two field situations are identical, most anthropologists will recognize themselves and their experience in this book.

GEORGE AND LOUISE SPINDLER

General Editors
Stanford, July 1965

PREFACE

In *Bunyoro: An African Kingdom* (hereafter referred to as *Bunyoro*) I gave an outline account, based on twenty-two months of fieldwork, of the social and cultural life of the Banyoro or Nyoro, a Bantu people of western Uganda. Here I describe how that study was made. As my account is centrally concerned with the particularities of Bunyoro and of my work there, it is necessarily in large part autobiographical. If on this account it seems (as it does to me) to be a somewhat immodest undertaking, I can only plead that the idea was not mine but that of the Editors. Also, although I shall be talking mainly about my work in Bunyoro, I hope that what I say may have some bearing on wider problems of research in traditional, centralized societies of comparable type. The last thing I intend is to propose my field study as a model: I made errors of both commission and omission. But failures as well as successes can be instructive, and in what follows I try to take equal account of both.

I completed my fieldwork in Bunyoro a decade ago. But since then methods of field study have not changed very much in their essentials. If I were beginning my researches in Bunyoro now instead of a dozen years ago, I should adopt very much the same kinds of approaches, though of course I should have to take account of very different political conditions, and I should no doubt emphasize some problems more and some less than I did then. It remains as true in the 1960s as it was in the 1950s that the only way to acquire anything approaching a full understanding of a human community is to live in it for a year or more, to communicate with its members in their own tongue, and to get to know them as real human individuals.

I do not think that I need repeat here the acknowledgments made in my *Bunyoro* case study, except to reaffirm my deep and lasting obligation to the people of Bunyoro of all classes whose patience, cooperation, and good humor made my work in their country both possible and enjoyable; to the Treasury Committee for Studentships in Foreign Languages and Cultures, London, whose generosity enabled me to go there; to Professor Evans-Pritchard, who has read and commented helpfully on the present text; and to my wife, who had a part in it all.

JOHN BEATTIE

Oxford, England
July 1965

CONTENTS

UNDERSTANDING AN AFRICAN KINGDOM: BUNYORO

Preparation for Field Research

Introductory: Theoretical Training

THE PRESENT STUDY falls naturally into three parts. In this chapter I deal briefly with preparation for field research; in the second, third, and fourth chapters, which form the core of the book, I describe my work in the kingdom of Bunyoro itself; and in the fifth and final chapter I discuss the last and perhaps the most difficult stage of research, that of writing up and publishing one's material.

In 1939 Audrey Richards wrote:

> It is impossible to write a "purely descriptive account" of any human culture, however simple. The facts recorded are themselves the result of selection, conscious or unconscious, in accordance with the observer's interests or theoretical outlook, even if he refrains from putting any special interpretation on these facts. (Richards 1939)

It follows from this clear statement that the student who wishes, nowadays, to make a field study of an unfamiliar culture must undergo an intensive course of specialist training if his work is to be taken seriously by other scholars. In the last half century or so social anthropology has come of age; it has grown into a distinct specialist subject with a specific body of theory and with a vast and rapidly expanding range of comparative ethnography at its disposal. At an earlier period there was little difference between the amateur and the professional, for there was no such developed and systematic body of knowledge about other cultures, especially preliterate and non-Western ones. It is true that many of the first important studies of simpler, smaller-scale societies were made by missionaries and administrators without specialist training. But today this is no longer possible.

The difference is not just between approaching the data with a theory or theories about them and approaching them with an open mind, empty of prejudices or preconceived ideas. Nobody can undertake any kind of investigation with a completely blank mind, lacking any notion of what he is trying to find out or of how he should go about his task. Any thinking about or observation of anything is guided by categories and ideas. The crucial question is rather whether these ideas are simply unanalyzed "common-sense" ones, or whether they are explicit, articulate, and reflect the kinds of problems and interests presently current in the field of enquiry concerned. Like any other sort of scientific investigation fieldwork in social anthropology is an attempt to solve problems, and it is easy to see that such an attempt is more likely to be successful if the investigator has some idea of what the problems are.

Perhaps it is not quite so evident why the social anthropologist's questions should not derive simply from the familiar and homely categories of "common sense." Why should he have to master a great deal of sociological theory and comparative ethnography before he goes to the field? But on a little reflection the answer is plain. All science begins in "common sense"; but it does not stop there. As more and more information in a particular area of human knowledge is collected, and as the intricacy of these data comes to be better understood, the kinds of questions that the investigator asks necessarily become more and more specialized, and less and less obvious to the layman. (This is not to say that they should not and cannot, at some later stage, be made intelligible to laymen.) Just as an explorer cannot publish a scientifically adequate description of a hitherto unknown plant species without some knowledge of botany, so an investigator cannot describe—or, often, even understand—an unfamiliar social or cultural institution without some knowledge of social anthropology. For the sociological fieldworker the situation is still further complicated by the fact that his task is not just to describe an unfamiliar institution from the outside in terms of his own culture; he must learn to see it, and the whole social and cultural world of which it is a part, as far as possible as it appears to the members of that culture themselves. This means that he must learn to think in the categories of the people he is studying as well as in his own, and this is never a simple task. Among other things it requires that the investigator acquire a sufficient knowledge of that people's language; and it requires, no less, than he be adequately trained in social anthropology.

Emphases in social anthropological training vary from country to country, but it is fair to say that, until recently at least, the emphasis in most British university departments has been on social structure. Very briefly, this means that students trained in Great Britain have been taught to think largely in terms of social institutions, that is, of the systems of institutionalized social relationships customary between different categories or groups of persons in a society. Such are the relationships between parents and children, husbands and wives, rulers and subjects, producers and consumers, and so on, in a particular society. But the structurally trained anthropologist does not study these institutions in isolation from one another; an essential part of his approach is that he should regard them functionally, that is, that he should look for the ways in which they interact in the society he is studying. Thus he may investigate systematically the connection between kinship and ritual activity, for example, or the implications of a particular system of political authority for the mode of territorial distribution, or the type of land holding. There are many examples of such correlations in modern ethnography.

But this "structural-functional" concern does not preclude the investigation of people's concepts, beliefs, and values, material usually regarded as cultural. And it has become increasingly clear in recent years that the study of human social institutions in either structural-functional causal terms, or in cultural, ideal terms, necessarily requires constant reference from one level to the other. Accounts of the character and development of social anthropology in Britain are available elsewhere (*cf.,* for example, Evans-Pritchard 1951, Lienhardt 1964, Beattie 1964): I refer to the subject here because the theoretical basis for my Bunyoro study derived mainly from this kind of training, undertaken entirely at the graduate level. (Before becoming an anthropologist I had graduated in philosophy, and then spent eight years in Tanganyika as an administrator.) My prefieldwork training consisted of a year's intensive reading for the Oxford Diploma in Anthropology, centrally in social anthropology, but at that time including also some physical anthropology and prehistory, followed by a further year spent writing a thesis for the Bachelor of Letters degree. At that stage my own main interests were in the political institutions of smaller-scale societies in general, and of traditional African states in particular: my thesis was on traditional checks on the abuse of political power in four such states, Buganda, Swazi, Ashanti, and Nupe, of which there were more or less adequate accounts in the literature (my conclusions were later published in Beattie 1959).

While working for my Bachelor of Letters degree I had been considering fieldwork possibilities, and also, as students must, possible sources of financial support. I decided to work, if I could, in the interlacustrine Bantu area of East Africa, one of the most densely populated regions in the continent, which contains a number of other large and important traditional states besides Bunyoro. Also, I applied for and was fortunate enough to be awarded a Senior Studentship by the Treasury Committee for Studentships in Foreign Languages and Cultures, London. As well as meeting certain lesser expenses the Committee granted me a basic allowance of £500 per annum, and I found this sum quite adequate to my needs in the field.

Choice of Area and Preparation for the Field

Bunyoro was not my first choice. I had originally hoped to study the relatively unknown and politically less developed Ha people of northwestern Tanganyika. But I found that another anthropologist had already chosen that area to work in. So although Bunyoro was by no means *terra incognita* (it had been briefly studied by the missionary John Roscoe in the twenties), I accepted—with perhaps a twinge of regret that I should not be tilling ethnographically virgin soil—the suggestion of the then director of the East African Institute of Social Research at Makerere, Dr. Audrey Richards, that I should undertake my research there.

My decision, which I have never regretted, was based on a number of grounds. I knew that although Bunyoro lies in the north of the interlacustrine region, it was and had been for many generations one of the most influential kingdoms in the area, as well as being probably the oldest, so that a thorough modern study of it might be relevant to other later studies in the same part of Africa. Its ethnographic importance had been stressed by Dr. W. E. H. Stanner in his invaluable *Report on Social Science Research in Uganda and Tanganyika* (1949, unpublished). He had written that "of the six larger tribes [in the inter-lacustrine region] the four on which additional and more up-to-date information is badly needed are the Soga, Nyoro, Toro and Gishu." He went on to say that "social change among the closely related Nyoro and Toro is in some ways far advanced and unless one or the other (preferably the Nyoro, the larger) is studied in detail within the next few years the chance to record their traditional life may well have passed well beyond its best." The events of the past decade or so have amply vindicated Stanner's judgment, and his remarks impressed me particularly because I retained from my years as an administrator a special inter-est in social change, and especially in the effects of European overrule on indige-nous political institutions. Finally, although Roscoe's book (1923) was and still is an indispensable source, it is old-fashioned and superficial by modern stan-dards, being based not on long residence and intensive research, but on a rela-tively brief visit and on set questions to informants, put for the most part through interpreters. (I should say that these strictures do not apply to Roscoe's great study of the neighboring people, *The Baganda*.) So when I decided on Bun-yoro I knew that it was a traditional African state of major importance, that like the rest of Africa it was undergoing rapid and accelerating social change, and that no fully adequate study of it existed. These, I felt, were good enough rea-sons to justify my choice.

The fact that Bunyoro was already well known to the Western world (Eu-ropean contact had begun in 1862 and there had been European missionaries and a settled administration in the country for more than half a century) meant that I could learn a good deal about it before I went there. In addition to Ros-coe's book there were numerous references to Bunyoro in the writings of Vic-torian and later travelers and explorers, such as Speke, Grant, Baker, Emin Pasha, and many others, and in books and reports by administrators and mis-sionaries. So once my decision was made I spent much time in libraries learning from these sources as much as I could about the country and its people.

Another consequence of Bunyoro's long contact with Christian missions was that its language, one of the four major tongues of the interlacustrine area, was fairly, though by no means completely, adequately recorded. Like most modern social anthropologists I was determined from the beginning to work through the native tongue and not through interpreters. This task was made much easier for me than it is for many anthropologists (though I found it difficult enough!) by the fact that a published grammar and dictionary of the language already existed, compiled by members of the Church Missionary Soci-ety, which had been long established in the area, as well as two or three short books written in Lunyoro by Nyoro themselves, mostly about the history and traditions of their country. I possessed the further advantage of having a good working knowledge of another, though quite different, Bantu language, Kiswahili, acquired as a district officer in Tanganyika. I found that a few Nyoro could speak some Swahili, but, more important, the grammatical structure of Lunyoro, involving like other Bantu languages a complex system of noun classes and concords, was reassuringly familiar. To all these advantages was added the further benefit of a few weeks' tuition at the School of Oriental and African Studies in London from Professor A. N. Tucker, with the help of a Nyoro speaker from Uganda. But in spite of this flying start I found, as will appear, the job of gaining a good working knowledge of the language in the field an exceedingly arduous one. I might have found it a little easier if I had at an earlier stage had fuller and more detailed instruction in elementary linguistics, now generally regarded as an essential part of the training of any social anthropologist who intends to work in a culture with a language radically different from his own.

On just how when one got to the field one went about one's task, on the practical techniques which would be useful in collecting the kinds of information I wanted, I was perhaps less adequately informed. It was unusual in English anthropology courses at that time (it still is) to give very detailed formal instruction on methods of field research. Sometimes, indeed, one rather got the impression that fieldwork was simply a matter of getting into the field and being there; once there one would absorb information by a kind of osmosis, helped, no doubt, by that invaluable vade-mecum, *Notes and Queries on Anthropology*. There are, I think, merits in this somewhat casual "sink or swim" approach, at least in the context of teaching at Oxford, where students are discouraged from going to the field until they have completed at least two years of graduate study, by which time they may be expected to show a certain maturity and judgment. It means that the fieldworker has to work out his own techniques when he gets there, and it avoids the danger of the too doctrinaire adoption of methods that are appropriate in one culture, but may be less, or not at all, so in another. Also, in most graduate teaching departments there is a good deal of contact, both formal and informal, between students who have just returned from the field and those who have not yet gone there, and much, though not all, can be learned from other people's experience. Again, though few social anthropologists have recorded in detail how they carried out their fieldwork, and fewer still have discussed the problems of fieldwork in general (Audrey Richards, whom I quoted at the beginning of this chapter, is one of the exceptions), passing references to fieldwork problems and the manner in which they were dealt with do occur in many anthropological monographs. Finally, and most important of all, a firm line cannot be drawn between theory and fieldwork; we saw that there can be no fieldwork without theory, and the converse is equally true, for if theory is to be of any use it must be grounded in empirical study. So much theoretical writing has an important bearing on fieldwork practice.

Malinowski's contribution in this respect has been especially important, and his own brilliant fieldwork and that of his pupils (who compose most of the senior generation of present-day social anthropologists in Britain) bear witness to the fruitfulness of his teaching. For him a human culture was an organic unity, "a connected living whole with the three dimensions of social organization, material outfit, and belief." The "isolates" of culture were institutions, each of which, in Malinowski's rather idiosyncratic use of the term, had "its personnel (social structure), its charter (or values), its norms, activities and material equipment" (Kaberry 1957). Every culture must thus exhibit a range of institutions, each directed towards the achieving of some end or ends conceived to be important in that culture. We need not here consider Malinowski's theoretical development of this schema in his theory of biological needs, but from the point of view of fieldwork it is plain that this way of characterising institutions could provide the basis for a comprehensive set of headings and subheadings under which field data could be systematically organized. In the context of a particular culture such a schema could of course, to begin with, be only provisional, subject to constant review and reformulation. But even though some headings might prove to be redundant, and new ones would certainly be needed, this approach at least helped to ensure that little that was important was left out and that full account was taken of the culture in the round.

On my way to Bunyoro in 1951 I spent a few weeks at the East African Institute of Social Research at Makerere, Kampala (I was associated either informally or, later, formally with the Institute throughout my fieldwork, in which, as will become evident, it and its director played an important part), and I was fortunate in having such a Malinowskian "cultural outline" made available to me there. This outline, not, I believe, published either then or since, provided a number of heads and subheads under which data could be assembled. If, as often happens, the same material fell appropriately under more than one heading it could readily be cross-referenced. Typical broad headings were Environment, History, Material Culture, Political Structure, Legal Rules and Norms, Values; and each of these was subdivided into a number of subheadings. Thus "Legal Rules and Norms" might be subdivided into (a) rules relating to kinship (marriage, inheritance, succession, parental responsibility, and so on); (b) rules relating to political activity (legal rights and duties of headmen, subchiefs and chiefs, rules of appointment to office, and such like), (c) social sanctions: legal, organized, diffuse (public opinion); and under a number of other subheadings. It is easy to see that much material collected under one of these subheads might equally well be included under other heads. Thus norms of family obligation might fall, also, under the heading of "values"; rules of succession to political authority would be relevant also under the heading of "political organization," and so forth.

In this way the fieldworker is encouraged to keep constantly in mind the possible implications for one another of the various institutions he studies. So he learns to think of culture not as "a thing of shreds and patches" but as in some sense a systematic whole made up of interconnected parts (though of course he would be wrong to assume that this "whole" is necessarily either harmonious or well ordered). This Malinowskian approach may also ensure that no theme of major importance is forgotten and omitted altogether. As a prescription for the initial stages of fieldwork there is much to be said for it, if intelligently used.

So before I left Kampala for the field, I had provided myself with some dozens of strong paper file covers, labelled with the heads and subheads that I hoped might be appropriate to the Nyoro case. Of course I realized that these headings would certainly need a good deal of revision once I had got to know something about Nyoro culture: they did. But I hoped that at least they would enable me to start collecting material in a reasonably systematic way right from the beginning, and this they did too.

Of more strictly material and personal preparations for fieldwork I need not say much here. I had the advantage of already knowing East Africa well, and so it was easy for me to assess the minimum of personal effects that I should need. I knew that I should be living, either in a tent or a hut, with and among the people, and so would need basic camp and cooking equipment—much of this I possessed already. I knew that there were hospitals and dispensaries in Bunyoro (though few and far between), so that I did not need to worry about basic medical supplies. I also knew that Bunyoro covered an area of about 4700 square miles and had an adequate road system, so that some form of transport would be essential. I began my fieldwork with a hired lorry; later I took over a used station wagon from a fellow Treasury student who had completed his research in another part of Africa.

It had seemed best to leave my wife and three-year-old son at home in Oxford for the initial period of my fieldwork, so that I could "break the ice"— learn the language, choose a place to live, and so on—before they joined me. In the end this turned out to be wise: however devoted an anthropologist is, unless he is a far better linguist than I am, the task of gaining fluency in a foreign language as rapidly as possible will be much easier if for some months he is compelled to use, or attempt to use, that language only.

So one day toward the end of September 1951 I set off on the 130-mile trip from Kampala to Hoima, Bunyoro's capital and the residence of the king or Mukama and of the district commissioner and his headquarters staff. With me I had a temporary cook whom I had employed in Kampala (I soon replaced him in Bunyoro by a native Nyoro speaker), my camping equipment, my files and notebooks, a portable typewriter, a camera, and a (very) few books. My fieldwork was about to begin.

2

The First Six Months

Early Contacts

I SPENT altogether nineteen months in Bunyoro during the years 1951–1953, and a further three months there in 1955. These nineteen months were divided into two periods, separated by an interval of four months during which I returned to Oxford. As my problems, preoccupations, and techniques were quite different in each of these periods, I deal in this chapter with the first, leaving the more broadly based preoccupations of my second and longer tour of fieldwork for the next two chapters.

My most immediate tasks after I arrived in Bunyoro were two. First, I wanted to meet the most important people in Bunyoro (or some of them), the men with most authority, on whose good will and cooperation I would sooner or later be dependent, and from whom I might hope to gain as quickly as possible a general, though not necessarily accurate, picture of Bunyoro and its people. This meant that I had to see a number of locally important Europeans, as well as the traditional Nyoro authorities. Although Bunyoro was still a traditional kingdom, it had been governed under a European administration and much influenced by European missionaries for more than half a century, and these factors, I knew, must have vastly altered its traditional character and constitution. What I had to study was not an untouched, purely "African" state; rather it was a community and polity in which traditional and modern Western elements were inextricably confused. My field, in short, was not any kind of static society, but one in process of rapid social change and "culture contact," a process in which the Europeans were the major agents. And my main task, as I saw it, was to understand Bunyoro as it was in 1951, not to attempt to reconstruct a traditional culture and society that no longer existed.

The second thing I had to decide, partly on the basis of the advice I might receive from the authorities I consulted, was whereabouts in Bunyoro I should start my intensive fieldwork. So for the first fortnight I stayed at the district headquarters at Hoima, first at the government resthouse, then, through the courtesy of the district commissioner, in a temporarily vacant government quarter.

My first call was on the European district commissioner, who, under the provincial commissioner, was in charge of the Bunyoro district. He was helped by two assistant district officers, one at Hoima and one posted to Masindi, who were British like himself, and by a staff of Asian and African clerks, interpreters, and messengers. The Protectorate government was also represented at Hoima by medical, agricultural, and police officers.

From the district commissioner, as from his assistants and successors, I received throughout my stay much cooperation and help (I give some instances later), as well as personal hospitality. The social anthropologist working in an administered area soon learns how much he depends on the good will of the administration, whether this be European, as it was then in Bunyoro, or indigenous, as it is now. He should therefore establish good relations with local officialdom as quickly as he can. Fortunately I already realized this; as a district officer in Tanganyika I had had experience of the presence of "outside" research workers in areas for which I was responsible, and of the kinds of demands which they sometimes make. Accordingly I took pains to explain to the district commissioner, and also to the other district officials I met, what kind of research I hoped to undertake in the district, and, in broad terms, how I proposed to go about it.

But it is vital for the anthropologist to establish and retain, as far as he can, a reputation for impartiality and disinterestedness among the people he is working with, and especially to avoid identification with the "government." This was particularly important in Bunyoro. For very good historical reasons (set out in Chapter 2 of *Bunyoro*) there was a widespread if rarely explicit resentment and distrust of Europeans in general, and of their Protectorate government in particular. Thus too overt an association with the European administration, especially at the outset, would have been disastrous for my work. I therefore declined invitations, for example, to join the European officials and their families at tennis during my first two weeks at Hoima; I also declined a pressing and well-meant suggestion by the district commissioner that I should accompany him on a tour of the district for several days, so that he could introduce me to some of the county and subcounty chiefs. I explained to him that such an introduction to the rural areas in which I hoped to work would be fatal to my research, but I am not sure that he was completely convinced.

My next call was on the Mukama, the traditional ruler of Bunyoro and the head of its native government. His palace, called Karuzika, is about a mile from the district office, and the headquarters of the native government were a hundred yards or so from the palace (they have since been moved). In 1951 the Mukama, who is a man of considerable dignity and presence, was about sixty-five years old. At that time he wielded a great deal more power than he does now, especially in matters concerning the appointment, dismissal, and promotion of his territorial chiefs. Unless he approved my research the indispensable cooperation of the local authorities throughout the country would not have been forthcoming. In my conversation with him, conducted in English, I stressed particularly my concern with Nyoro history: I knew that this was a central interest of his own, as he had published three articles in the *Uganda Journal* on the origins and traditional history of his own dynasty. But I also explained that I was interested as well in present-day Nyoro society and culture. Like others, he found this interest rather less comprehensible.

A central theme in our discussion was whether I should begin my study at the capital, Hoima, or in a rural area some distance from the center. This is a major question for any social anthropologist who undertakes the over-all study of a centralized society. The Mukama pointed out, as did others also, that the people who knew most about Nyoro history and traditions were himself and his advisers, and he suggested that if this was what I wanted to learn about, it would be much more sensible for me to stay at Hoima, instead of setting up camp far away in the bush among a lot of uneducated peasants. However, I had been taught that the proper way to do fieldwork was to settle down in a small-scale community, and by working through the language, by observation, and by participation in its daily activities over a considerable period of time, by becoming in short a member of it, to get to know it well from the inside. It was plain to me that I could not do this in Hoima, surrounded by important officials, many of them English-speaking, and in constant contact with the European community. If I wanted to learn what life was like for ordinary Nyoro, to speak their language fluently, and to get to know them as people, I would evidently have to do so in the country and not in the town. The Mukama thought this point of view somewhat eccentric; also, there would have been advantages from his point of view in having this obviously inquisitive stranger within reach, where an eye could be kept on his activites. Nevertheless he accepted my decision, once made, and as I have acknowledged elsewhere I owe much to his and his native government's cooperation.

But the choice was a difficult one; either decision was bound to have drawbacks. By starting at the periphery and working in towards the center I inevitably caused the Mukama and his officials to wonder what I could possibly be up to. This, I believe, made them a little less anxious to help than they might otherwise have been when, in the second stage of my fieldwork, I did turn my attention to the center. For by that time I knew the language and the country well, and since no administration is without its seamy side, they knew that some of the things I had learned about (for example, certain aspects of the inner workings of local government) were not, at least to European eyes, wholly to their credit. In the next chapter I consider some of the difficulties to which this circumstance gave rise.

But I believe that my decision was the right one. For it was in fact possible to learn a great deal at the center after spending the first six months in the country, whereas it would, I think, have been impossible to learn anything of life at the grass-roots level if I had first lived for some months at the capital. For even though I had behaved oddly in choosing to go off to live in rural squalor when I might have resided comfortably in Hoima, and even though when I did come to live near Hoima I had, though by then reasonably fluent in the language, acquired a peasant accent and turn of speech, still, I did retain the prestige of being an educated European and by that time I had learned enough about Bunyoro to enable me to ask the right questions. If, however, I had attempted to study a rural Nyoro community after spending six months or so in Hoima, in close and open association with European officials and missionaries and with the Mukama and his advisers, I am sure that I would have found it impossible to win the confidence of members of the Nyoro peasant community, in the degree to which I did win it. An important factor here, though I did not at that time fully appreciate it, was the category distinction which Nyoro habitually make between "state" or "government" (*obukama* or *obulemi*) on the one hand, and "community" on the other; the two spheres are seen, at least from the bottom, as standing in opposition to each other. So I was wiser than I knew in feeling that it was essential for me as far as possible to avoid any identification in the eyes of the ordinary people with the European ascendancy, or with the central administration associated with it.

After visiting the Mukama, I was taken by the district commissioner to meet the chief minister of the native (now Kingdom) government, the Katikiro. At that time this office was held, in an acting capacity, by a very distinguished Nyoro, himself the author of an important study of Nyoro traditions and history. He seemed to be rather inhibited by the district commissioner's presence, but expressed doubt that I would learn anything of interest in his country and was surprised when I said that I hoped to learn the language within a year. However he agreed to see me again, alone, a few days later, and then he was more forthcoming. In the course of an hour's conversation, mostly in Kiswahili, as his English was weak, he told me much of recent Nyoro history. The Nyoro, he said, were a dying race (I was impressed then, as later, by the way in which the almost universally derogatory European stereotype of the Nyoro people had come to be reflected in their image of themselves); their spirit was broken. *"Roho imekufa,"* he said, in Kiswahili, literally "their soul has died." The reasons for this, he explained, were the seizure of Nyoro cattle by the British in their campaign against Bunyoro in the late nineties, the theft of a large and important part of Bunyoro (the "Lost Counties") at the same period and its incorporation in Buganda, and the refusal of the Protectorate government to allow Nyoro to hold their land in freehold tenure like the Ganda (*cf. Bunyoro,* pp. 22–23). However the Katikiro also made some useful suggestions as to possible places where I might start my fieldwork.

During my first few days in the country I also called on the heads of the two Christian churches then active in Bunyoro, the Anglican Church Missionary Society and the Roman Catholic White Fathers. The acting head of the Church Missionary Society at that time was a Nyoro priest, from whom I received some useful information, and also some helpful advice about possible sites in which to begin work. From the European Father Superior at the White Fathers' Mission, who had spent many years in Bunyoro, I also learned a good deal, not least of his view of the Nyoro, which reflected the now familiar European stereotype. A transcription of my diary entry for that day will give the flavor of our talk:

> In afternoon called on local White Fathers—had a long talk with Fr. Superior ———, who has been in Bunyoro for x years. Expressed himself strongly on apathy, idleness, and general decadence of Banyoro (he can't get labor to finish his church), their immaturity, superstition, etc. Criticised C.M.S. for employing African teachers—as witch-ridden as their pupils, he said. As sample of their [Nyoro's] stupidity he mentioned their belief that the Bazungu [Europeans] had taken their cattle away from them (they died of rinderpest mostly), that injections were given for the purpose of depriving them of *akili* [intelligence], and that Europeans in general were concerned to do them down, a belief, he said, fostered by mysterious agents "from elsewhere." Morals were at a low ebb, he said, 95 percent (?) were syphilitic, and most are in the hands of witchdoctors who mulct them of their money. He mentioned also the fact (already mentioned by A.D.C.) that native medical staff charge heavily for medicine (and added that there was a high attendance at the Sisters' dispensary). Too many Africans with a smattering of English fancy themselves educated (though the Brother in charge of the school said that there was a "back to the land" tendency). Regretted decline of corporal punishment and referred to increase of theft since ancient penalty (cutting off ear, finger, and lips) done away with. Repeated several times that the country was going down—going from bad to worse.

I may say that I took all this with a grain of salt, for the old Father did not seem unduly distressed at having spent his life at so hopeless and useless a task as trying to improve such a people.

During this period I also met the European agricultural officer, who unlike most local Europeans had a genuine interest in the native culture (he had made a study of local plant names and uses), the medical officer, the police officer, and the provincial commissioner at Masindi, and I learned something from them all.

I had also, by now, returned my temporary cook to Kampala (he had come with me on that understanding), and had engaged a local Nyoro in this capacity. I interviewed several men, some with excellent references, before engaging Yositasi (Eustace); and it is worth recording that ability as a cook was only one—perhaps not the most important—of the qualities I was looking for. I knew that I and the man I took on would be living in quite close companionship in the bush for long periods, and that at least in the early stages of my work I would be dependent on him for much more than just food: for helping me in my initial contacts with the local people, for example, and for advice on matters of etiquette. So I needed someone who was prepared to live in camp conditions, who spoke some Kiswahili, and who was also intelligent, cheerful, and gregarious. Yositasi certainly had these qualities, if at times he was temperamental. He was also a brilliant raconteur and mimic, and often regaled me (and later my wife) in the evenings with highly dramatized accounts of his adventures and encounters in his earlier career as cook at a European resthouse in a neighboring district.

In addition to Yositasi I engaged a second and junior "boy," very much as Yositasi's subordinate and second in command. This was a matter of status rather than of domestic need; without this minimal domestic staff I would have been regarded, in status-conscious Bunyoro, as either too poor or too mean to support such dependents, and this would have hindered rather than helped my research.

Selection of Site

On the basis of the various suggestions made to me I had by this time listed a number of possible places to settle in and start intensive research, and I spent several days driving about the country in my hired truck, interviewing the county and subcounty chiefs of the areas I was considering, and being taken by them to possible sites. I took a good deal of time and care in coming to what was obviously going to be an important decision, and in reaching it I had four major criteria especially in mind.

First, the community I settled in had to be, so far as I could judge, a reasonably representative one; as typical as possible of rural Bunyoro. Of course I could not at that time know with certainty exactly what *was* typical, but at least I could exclude from consideration areas that were obviously not so; those which were close to and therefore affected by either of Bunyoro's two towns, for example, or which neighbored one of the country's few nonnative estates, or which contained, as one or two areas did, significantly large groups of non-Nyoro. Also, I made a point of seeking an area of reasonably lengthy occupation; in a newly settled area long-established local ties of kinship and neighborhood would be lacking, and most such relationships as there were would lead outside the area altogether.

Secondly, my chosen area had to be reasonably remote not only from Hoima, but also from the local county or subcounty chief's headquarters. These were generally on or near main roads, and to have lived too close to one, with its office and court and, sometimes, its English-speaking clerks, would have made direct contact with the rural community itself more difficult. These chiefs represented "state" rather than "community," and I had realized already that for my preliminary community study it was important to avoid too close identification with any center of official authority. I wished, also, to be far enough away from a main road and sufficiently inaccessible to discourage the constant "dropping in" of European officials and others on tour, which would similarly have defeated my purpose.

At the same time, thirdly (and not perhaps wholly consistently with the foregoing), my base had to be accessible, if not too easily so, by motor vehicle, so that I could move my equipment there, obtain supplies and mail, and maintain some contact with the outside world without undue difficulty and expense. And lastly, and most importantly of all, I wanted to find an area where not only did the local subcounty chief and his headmen seem to be reasonably cooperative and to have some understanding of what I was aiming to do, but also where the people themselves (a representative group of whom were summoned by the local chief to meet me in each of the areas I visited) seemed willing to put up with an intrusive European and even to help him in his task.

At all the places I visited I explained through the chief what I was there for. My speech to the assembled villagers would run something like this:

> I have come to your country to learn your language, and about your history, your traditions and your customs, and the way you live. I have come from a big school in Europe where grown-ups are taught, including some who will come to Africa. Many Europeans are very ignorant about the customs of Africans; if they are taught properly about these things before they come here, perhaps they will be more tolerant and less repressive than some have been in the past. I have nothing to do with the government and I am not a missionary. I have not come here to order you around or to tell you what you should do. I have come as a pupil and not as a teacher, but I can only learn if you will allow me to live with you and if you will be my teachers.

And so on. This speech (it would have to be somewhat rephrased today) was for the most part received with amused incredulity. But nowhere was any overt opposition expressed (perhaps because my claims were usually strongly supported by the chief), and in several places people seemed willing, even pleased, at the idea of having a resident European come to live with them; partly, no doubt, because at least he might turn out to be an economic asset to the community.

I soon decided to base myself in the area of the subcounty chief of Mutuba IV in Bugahya county, about thirty miles southwest of Hoima. Most of this area had been settled a long time, and there were no Europeans and few non-Nyoro living in it. The local chief was intelligent and cooperative (though jumpy and quick tempered; I later found that he was locally known as *ndabukya* —a quick, clever person, rather lacking in dignity; the term is slightly pejorative), and he seemed quickly to grasp what I was attempting to do. After visiting and considering several areas in his subchiefdom I finally settled on the *ekyaro* or settlement area of Kihoko, about three miles distant from the subchief's headquarters, along a barely motorable track through tall elephant grass and bush (I had to cut out a number of large tree stumps before I could use it safely) that petered out in the settlement. Kihoko satisfied all four of my desiderata: it was representative and long settled; the only non-Nyoro in its population of 150 or so were two Nilotic settlers from northern Uganda; it was reasonably, but not too, remote and difficult of access; and the people seemed well disposed. Also, the local subcounty chief was cooperative even to the point of embarrassment; he was almost too anxious to help by ordering the local people to assist me in every possible way and bossing them around. But I never regretted this choice of area, nor the trouble I took in making it.

The next thing to do was to choose a camp site and move in. The choice of a site in countries like Bunyoro offers more difficulties than it does in communities that live in real "villages," for where households are not grouped together but dispersed one cannot acquire a house or erect one's tent in the middle of the village and by simply sitting in one's doorway observe the daily activities of village life. In Bunyoro households are scattered fairly evenly throughout the settled areas and are separated from one another by distances that vary from a few score yards to a quarter of a mile or more. And not only this, but also all land not under cultivation is covered for most of the year by a dense stand of elephant grass from six to ten feet or more high, so that one household is rarely even visible from another, though it may be audible. I had originally hoped to establish myself in or adjoining the courtyard of a friendly and typical household, but this was impracticable because no one was willing to take the risk of having a strange European right on his doorstep: even a Nyoro would not have built his house cheek by jowl with a stranger. So I settled for a spot, with one or two shade trees, about seventy yards from my nearest neighbor, who seemed willing to have me there. (I learned afterwards, however, that he had been strongly advised to abandon his house and build elsewhere after I had decided on this site.) This was just beyond the end of the motorable track, and involved cutting a hundred yards or so of new "road" through the bush and tall grass, and clearing the site itself. This task was accomplished in a day by me, my domestic staff of two, the subcounty chief, and about a dozen of my new neighbors.

The next day we built two small grass huts, one for me to sleep and work in, about ten feet by eight feet, and another, slightly smaller, for my staff; I added a borrowed tent a few weeks later.

Though ignorant of the technique of building with poles and grass, I was at least able to join the pole-cutting party and to help cut and transport (on my shoulders, which were bruised and painful for several days afterwards) the long poles from a stand in the bush about a mile distant. This was the first stage in my attempt to establish myself as a bona fide "villager," willing, unlike other Europeans, to live with them so far as they would allow on terms of equality. (This equality was not and could never become complete, for reasons which will become plain later.) The apparently willing cooperation of my neighbors in the job of housebuilding was no doubt partly due to the exhortations of my officious but, by now, enthusiastic friend the subcounty chief. But it owed something also, I think, to my promise that when the work was done I would provide a "house-warming" beer party for everyone. I had already ordered six large earthenware jars of banana beer, each jar containing four gallons or more, from a neighbor whose bananas were ripe; the beer takes four days to prepare (see *Bunyoro,* Chapter 6, for an account of its preparation and social importance).

The next day my camp was ready, and I moved in. At about 2 P.M. the beer arrived and the party began. At its height some fifty or more people—men, women, and children—were present. There was music (singing, drums, and a one-stringed "fiddle" or *ndingidi*) and dancing. The noise was tremendous, but I was impressed then, as at many later beer drinks, by the fact that there was practically no rowdiness or drunkenness or other unpleasant behavior. At the end an impromptu speech of welcome was made by a barely sober old man who was evidently held in some respect (I found out much later that he was a well-known diviner); among other things he admonished me not to make friends with the local women. I reassured him.

Settling In

Thus, quite auspiciously, my six-month residence in Kihoko began. In the rest of this chapter I give some account, without specific chronological reference, of the various problems of initiating research in the field and of the ways in which I attempted to solve them. At this point my immediate objectives were limited but quite clear. I wanted to acquire fluency in the language, to get to know the people of Kihoko, their mutual interrelationships and their way of life, as well as I could. At this stage I used no paid interpreters or informants, I carried out no surveys or censuses, and I made no use of set interviews or questionnaires. I felt, I believe rightly, that my first task was simply to get to know people and to learn how to converse with them, to acquire some grasp of their day-to-day interests and values, and above all to attempt to overcome their deep and very natural suspicion of me as a European; all the rest could come later. I found this task quite enough.

It had, as I saw it, three interrelated aspects. The first was to attempt to get myself accepted as a new and hitherto unknown species of European, a social anthropologist, to whom new kinds of responses might be appropriate, different from those appropriate to other Europeans. My second and connected task was to make plain, by giving help to people when it was needed and when it was practicable to do so, that I had some neighborly concern for my new neighbors, and was not there just to exploit them as informants while remaining indifferent to them as human beings. And the third and central aspect of my work in Kihoko, to which the first two were to contribute, was to open, advance, and sustain communication with as many people as possible. Here language was evidently basic, but no less crucial was the attempt to extend within the community my field of interpersonal social relationships. Though these several preoccupations overlap at many points, it will be simplest to deal with them separately.

My first job, then, was to get myself more or less accepted, and to overcome people's natural suspicion and distrust of me as a European. There were good reasons (given in Chapter 2 of *Bunyoro*) why there should be such distrust. In Bunyoro, as in other parts of what was then colonial Africa, Europeans had always been regarded as powerful outsiders, having skills and claiming status far higher than any African, and altogether remote from the local community. But, more than this, Nyoro believed that European soldiers and administrators had been responsible for the dismemberment and impoverishment of their country and the destruction of their cattle (to the benefit of their hereditary enemies the Ganda), and for reducing them to a state of permanent and galling subjection. The European missionaries who followed had, Nyoro thought, completed this work by disparaging and, with government support, attempting to extirpate traditional Nyoro religious practices, which as well as being much concerned with fertility (a natural preoccupation where illness is common and often fatal, and many children die in infancy), also played a vital part in the maintenance of traditional group values from the family upwards. And indeed it is true that indigenous ritual and religious cults were suppressed with quite exceptional rigor, perhaps partly because of the unusually close association between the Anglican missionaries and the native government during the early days of British administration. For ordinary Nyoro peasants, many of whom had never seen a European close up and most of whom had certainly never spoken to one, there *were* only two categories of Europeans, government officials and missionaries, and with neither of these could they conceive themselves as dealing on terms of easy familiarity and friendship.

Although as an anthropologist much of my behavior obviously did not conform to pre-existing notions about Europeans (no European had ever hitherto settled down in a Nyoro community and tried to participate on as equal terms as possible in at least some areas of Nyoro village life) I did make a conscious effort to create a new category for myself as quickly as I could. My physical participation in housebuilding, for example, and my communal beer parties were at least partly aimed at this. Also, shortly after I had settled into camp, I announced that I proposed to clear and cultivate a plot of sweet potatoes for my own use, and I proceeded to do so on an adjoining plot of uncleared land. The first local reaction to this was incredulity, followed by amused but not unkindly derision. I can still vividly recall the shoulder-breaking effort of clearing the dense patches of elephant grass with a machete. But the actual hoeing, with a broad-bladed native hoe, was even worse, as the clayey soil was wet and heavy, and adhered tenaciously to the blade in large and sticky masses that were almost impossible to remove. Soon my hands were painfully blistered. But before long my neighbors came to my assistance and the work was quickly done. My crop was poor, but my efforts were not wasted, for the local people had learned that "their" European was different: the usual if not wholly accurate stereotype of a European in much of Africa is a person who never dirties his hands in physical toil. They had learned, too, that they could do something better than he could.

As another and somewhat less arduous contribution to the same end, I grew a luxuriant beard during these first few months (I shaved it off later); my not wholly frivolous reason for this was that since of the two formerly familiar categories of Europeans, government officers were known to drink (European) beer but rarely wore beards, and missionaries, though often bearded, rarely drank beer, a European who was both bearded and beer-drinking might be a little less readily assimilated to either of these pre-existing categories!

More seriously, I knew that the overcoming of suspicion would be a matter of degree and that it could never be complete. Indeed, as I recorded in *Bunyoro*, some people whom I knew well and counted as my friends nevertheless retained lingering doubts about my intentions and good faith for the whole length of my stay. But increasingly there were exceptions, and even if my acceptance in Kihoko was subject to some reservations, it was genuine as far as it went. It would have been idle to have hoped to be fully integrated into the Ki-hoko community; no anthropologist can be wholly assimilated to another culture, nor would it be a good thing if he were. I could not, for example, change the color of my skin; however close my relations with my neighbors I carried this badge of my Europeanness with me wherever I went. (I should say, however, that at no time did this difference between us appear to either me or, as far as I could judge, to my neighbors as of the least importance.)

Much more importantly, I could not conceal the fact that as a European I was vastly richer, both in privilege and in material goods, than my Kihoko neighbors. No anthropologist who dwells for any length of time in a technologically simple and "underdeveloped" peasant community, however plainly he chooses to live, can fail to be struck by the vast disparity between his and their equipment and resources. It befits him to be modest in the face of the remarkable adjustment that the members of such communities have made to such disabilities as poverty, inadequate housing, diet and sanitation, constant and debilitating illness, and a high rate of infant mortality. This state of affairs imposes certain moral obligations on the anthropologist. I return to this point below.

So the field anthropologist can never *quite* become one with the people he is studying; it would not be a good thing if he could. Stranger value can be an important asset. Sometimes people talk more freely about their relationships with their neighbors and kinsfolk to an outsider, who is not himself personally involved in these relationships. I have already touched on the difficulty, in highly stratified societies like Bunyoro, of avoiding a too close identification with one status, class, or social group, an identification that might make later work in a different group difficult or impossible. As I have said, I did not in the end wholly succeed in bridging the gap between the village community and the ruling "aristocracy." But I did maintain contact with the Mukama, his senior chiefs, and other important people at the capital, by letter and by occasional visits, during my early fieldwork. Even these contacts served to mark me off from my Kihoko neighbors, who of course had no such important connections.

I have just said that the fieldworker can hardly help feeling some human concern for the people he lives among, and this concern can express itself in various kinds of assistance that it is in his power to give. In rural Bunyoro I found that these were mainly medical or financial, or both combined. If I had had nothing else to do, and possessed the necessary skills and equipment, I could easily have spent several hours a day dealing with the variety of illnesses and minor injuries that afflicted the people of Kihoko and neighboring areas. The nearest dispensary was about seven miles away, the nearest hospital, at Hoima, more than thirty. However, partly in self-defense, I maintained only the most exiguous of pharmacopoeia (the most important items in it were magnesium sulphate, cough medicine, aspirin, quinine, and sulphathiazole), and I encouraged those who could to go to the dispensary. Even so, I (and, later, my wife) spent a good deal of time dosing the sick, and applying sulpha powder to the skin ulcers that afflicted many people, especially children, owing to dietary deficiencies. Also, possession of a motor vehicle meant that I was under constant pressure to take people who were feeble, incapacitated, or just lazy to the dispensary, sometimes to the hospital at Hoima. Although I did this many times in cases of emergency (or apparent emergency; once I traveled at some hazard several miles of barely-passable track in a rainstorm to rescue an allegedly dying baby, only to find it playing quite happily in the rain), I soon found it necessary to put aside a certain day each week for the dispensary trip. On the whole this worked quite well, though I was always amazed how my springs stood up to the human burden they had to carry.

Sometimes the problem was to try to convince a patient, usually an older man, that he would benefit by hospital treatment; often such people were afraid of what might happen to them in the Europeans' hospitals, from which it was known (or believed) that few returned alive. One of my successful efforts at persuasion was with a middle-aged neighbor and friend who was incapacitated and in great pain from long-standing gonorrhoea, whom I persuaded to accept a loan and to come to Hoima for treatment, which was at once successful. Another was with an older man, who had for years had such an enormous and grotesque hydrocele of the scrotum that he could not walk or even stand up. This man had to be persuaded, over a period of months, to undertake the journey to Masindi hospital (in my car) and thence to Kampala for an operation. In the end he agreed, and when I next saw him, many months later, he was completely cured. I was not always so successful, however. A very pleasant youth in Kihoko, whom I knew well, gradually began to show signs of mental disturbance, and eventually took to wandering about the country attacking people. Nothing I could say could persuade his relatives to let me take him to Hoima, and in the end he was kept bound hand and foot with rope in his hut, which, some months later, burned to the ground with him inside it.

I was sometimes asked for loans of small sums of money—often to meet the cost of medical treatment at the local dispensary (where it was supposed to be free) or at the White Sisters' Mission dispensary at Hoima, where it had to be paid for. I always met these requests when they were made by local people, and I was much impressed by the promptness and punctiliousness with which such loans were returned, usually with a small present of a chicken, some eggs, or a few vegetables in addition. I have referred already to the beer parties that I gave for my neighbors from time to time, though these were intended to establish and maintain good relations rather than merely as gifts, and in any case I received reciprocal invitations to my neighbors' beer parties. But these parties also involved the distribution of cigarettes (mostly the cheap local variety that I smoked myself) in considerable quantities: and most informants expected to be kept in smokes while talking to me. Other items that I distributed from time to time were pictures from old illustrated magazines, with which the district and assistant district commissioners were kind enough to keep me supplied and which were used for wall decoration, and—a further index of our differential standards of living—discarded food cans for use as drinking vessels; I soon learned to use only the kind of can opener that leaves a smooth edge to the tin.

Beginning Research

I now describe in more detail some of the methods I adopted in Kihoko to advance as quickly as possible my understanding of the language, the culture, and the people. I have already described my initial beer party, and on the principle that one of the best ways of getting to know people, in Bunyoro as elsewhere, is over a drink (and also because I enjoyed them) I gave a number of beer parties during my months in Kihoko and visited many more as a guest. But of course the majority of my sessions with the local people, whether in their houses or in mine, were "dry," although I was expected to dispense cigarettes when I smoked myself, which was most of the time. Nowadays only old people smoke the traditional long black clay pipes; all younger men, and many women, smoke cigarettes. The mode of smoking them, incidentally, provides an interesting if trivial index of social status. All Nyoro peasants smoke with the lighted end of the cigarette inside their mouths, thus both protecting it from the weather and avoiding wasting any of the smoke. The lower grades of chiefs, village headmen and "parish" chiefs, also usually smoke in this way. I acquired a certain proficiency in doing so myself. But no one of subcounty or county chief rank would think of smoking in this plebian fashion; they smoke with the lighted end outside, in the European manner.

At my first party I had announced that I would welcome as guests all who cared to visit me, and that I would much appreciate it if I might also call on my neighbors in their own homes. To both of these proposals all present had vociferously, and no doubt euphorically, agreed. Accordingly, during the first two or three weeks I was besieged with visitors, who came and greeted me politely, and sat in crowds in my grass hut for hours. Of course I could understand only an occasional word of what they said, but my cook Yositasi helped, when he had time and felt so disposed, to interpret into Swahili for me. They were, however, pleased to be shown the pictures in Roscoe's book *The Bakitara or Banyoro,* especially the frontispiece, a photograph of the redoubtable Mukama Kabarega (the father of the present king), who had fought the British in the war of the 1890s and had died in exile. I also amused those who would listen by reading to them extracts from a small collection of Nyoro fables published in Lunyoro, but whether they were more amused by the stories themselves or by my attempts to read Lunyoro it would be hard to say. Right from the start, when I could, I noted down people's names in a notebook that I kept as a "visitor's book," one name to a page; in this way I was able, as I came to know more about them, to build up small dossiers on each of my neighbors. I recorded such items as their distinctive features (if any; I have always found it hard to remember names, and, when I do remember them, to associate them with their owners), in what direction they lived, their clan membership, their kinship links with other neighbors, and so on. During this early period, visitors came thick and fast all day long. I remarked in my diary during the first week. "It looks as though during the daylight hours I won't have much time to myself!"

I need not have worried—at least not on this account. As I might have foreseen, visitors dropped off rapidly after the first few weeks, and although I returned the visits of most of my earlier guests, I still did not know enough Lunyoro to sustain any kind of conversation after the lengthy conventional greetings had been exchanged. I took long solitary walks, and spent many hours in my hut studying Lunyoro grammar, or just reading Shakespeare, or Proust's *A la Recherche du Temps Perdu* (in English)—my only nonanthropological literary resources. For the next three months or so progress was, or seemed to me to be, slow. I continued to visit and to be visited, though at a much slower tempo than at the beginning, and to work at the language, but for a long time I felt that fluency in Lunyoro and any real understanding of Nyoro culture were as far away as ever.

My halting enquiries into such matters as the clan system, ritual, domestic and intergroup relations were for the most part greeted with kindly derision, incredulity, or evasion. Answers to questions about ghosts, witchcraft, divination, and such topics were invariably that these things were unknown in Bunyoro, or if they had ever existed they had long since been abandoned, since everybody was Christian now. Even readings of selected passages from Evans-Pritchard's *Witchcraft, Oracles and Magic among the Azande* elicited no response.

One day my cook, overhearing me asking someone what his clan was, caused me some irritation by bursting into roars of laughter, doubling up, and slapping his thighs; when he recovered sufficiently to speak he told me that the only occasion on which a man would ask another what clan he belonged to was when he proposed to marry into that man's family (this, though disconcerting, was of course grist to my mill). I found at this stage that the only way I could ascertain a man's clan membership was to read through the list in Roscoe's book, and observe my hearer's reaction to the names read out. Sometimes three or four men would come into my hut at one time, settle themselves comfortably on the floor, light up my cigarettes, and carry out a long, animated, and (to me) unintelligible conversation among themselves; my occasional attempts to join in were evidently regarded as tiresome and unwarranted interruptions, and were for the most part ignored. I made most progress, I found, when I could get a visitor alone, so that he could talk without being overheard by others, but my early attempts to do this were often frustrated by a youth of low-grade intelligence who unfortunately lived nearby and who would sit silently in my hut for hours and hours tracing small circles in the dust on the earth floor with his big toe.

Most anthropologists working on their own in an alien culture go through this period of frustration, sometimes even of despair, at one time or another. It is not made any easier if change of climate and diet (though I ate some canned food I lived largely on locally grown beans, sweet potatoes, and bananas) have minor but irritating effects on one's health. It is at this stage that all the fieldworker's moral and physical resources have to be devoted to carrying on, however hopeless the prospect of making a breakthrough. But on balance I much enjoyed these early days of fieldwork and my moods of depression were for the most part fleeting. But they were none the less real, and the fieldworker in a remote and unfamiliar culture should be prepared for them. A few days' visit to Kampala in January also helped.

Toward the end of these first six months in Kihoko I began to realize that after all I had made some real progress. Though I still had a vast amount to learn, even about Kihoko, I could now use the language, if not fluently, at least well enough to ask the questions I wanted to ask and to understand the answers, and also to grasp some of the import of overheard conversations. Through my growing knowledge of Lunyoro, a few of the key categories in Nyoro thinking were becoming known to me (I return to this point later). I now knew many of the hundred or so inhabitants of Kihoko by name. I knew two or three dozens of them well as individual people, with distinctive characters, backgrounds and interests, and a few of them as real friends, with whom even today I maintain occasional contact. I had been given honorary membership in a Nyoro clan (the Ababopi) by a neighbor, formerly a school teacher, so that I had entered into a kind of quasi-kin relationship with him and his relatives. I had learned by both enquiry and observation the outlines of the kinship terminology and the usages associated with it, and I knew many of the kinship links that served to bind the people of Kihoko into a single community. I had learned something of the material and economic side of Nyoro village life: the crop cycle, techniques of cultivation, housebuilding, and animal husbandry (Nyoro keep goats, chickens, sometimes a few sheep; nowadays rarely cattle because of the prevalence of trypanosomiasis). Almost always questions about technology and material artifacts are those to which answers are most readily given. I had not yet made any major breakthrough in regard to the ritual side of traditional Nyoro life. Any concern with ghosts, spirits, and sorcerers was still denied, though a tiny breach in the wall of secrecy was made on Christmas day, when I attended the local mission church, a tiny edifice of mud and wattle, with a group of my friends, and understood enough of the lay preacher's sermon to gather that he was urging his congregation to abandon their *mbandwa* spirit seances (the traditional Nyoro mediumship cult) and instead to come to repair the thatch on the church roof, which certainly did need attention. My companions, whom after the service I naturally taxed with having denied what the preacher had asserted, were, however, unabashed, claiming that he must have been talking about some other community, unknown to them. Finally, I had intentionally made no effort to analyze the working of the centralized political system and its hierarchy of chiefs, though I had learned a good deal about its impact at the grass-roots level.

At the end of my first six months in the country, then, my knowledge of Bunyoro was manifestly fragmentary and incomplete. But I had made a beginning. I had a fair working understanding of the language, and I had at last reached the point where further improvement was noticeable and rapid. I had acquired a broad picture of Bunyoro's historical and ecological background, of Nyoro modes of livelihood, and of some of the main outlines of their culture, on the basis of which I could, later, develop more intensive study of certain of their characteristic social and cultural institutions. And I had succeeded in establishing a relationship of friendship and good will, and some degree of confidence in and acceptance of my good faith, in one Nyoro community. Since news travels fast in Bunyoro, I hoped that this relationship would later stand me in good stead in other parts of the country, and I was not disappointed. Though my study in depth had hardly begun, and most of my labeled folders were still pathetically empty, I felt that if I had not done as well as I had hoped, at least I had not done as badly as I had, in my gloomier moments, sometimes feared.

3

The Second Tour:
Fieldwork Methods

New Approaches: Use of Assistants
and Informants

I SPENT the next four months at Oxford, where I went carefully through my notes to determine what I knew and what I did not, discussed my work with my supervisor and others at the Institute, kept up my study of the language, and prepared a 10,000 word report for the Treasury Committee on my fieldwork to date and my future research plans.

At the end of July 1952 I returned to Bunyoro, this time accompanied by my wife and son. I now had rather different aims from those which I had had ten months earlier, and so a rather different program of research. I still intended to continue to deepen and broaden my understanding of community life in Kihoko and elsewhere, but I proposed now to pursue intensively certain specific structural and cultural themes. These included the relationships between the various grades of chiefs, the system of land tenure, the detailed working of the systems of kinship and affinity, the nature of the traditional ritual institutions, and others. The importance of some of these themes had been impressed on me during my first months in Kihoko, though I had not yet acquired much understanding of them. There is an important sense in which a culture itself dictates what the social anthropologist shall study and how he shall study it. For evidently the categories, concepts, and values that are dominant for the people being studied (and these can only be discovered with increasing familiarity with the language and the culture) must also assume major importance for the anthropologist.

So it was with me in Bunyoro. In Kihoko I had become familiar with terms like *obulemi* (government), *obuko* (in-law-ship), *mahano* (a kind of ritual power in things), and many others, which were constantly on people's lips.

Although as yet I understood little of their real significance, I knew that for Nyoro each must connote a wide range of socially and culturally important meanings. One implication of this for the second stage of my fieldwork was that I would have now to seek out people who would be most likely to be informed, and willing to talk, about these matters. I give some examples below of how I did this.

I and my family established ourselves, by courtesy of the Bunyoro Kingdom government with whom I had previously arranged it, in a former chief's house, once the headquarters of a county that had some years earlier been absorbed into a larger one. This house, built of mud and thatch, had four tiny rooms, and wooden doors and shutters. It was about three miles south of Hoima, on the top of a gentle hill, and pleasantly surrounded by short grass and shady trees. Around it were scattered, rather more densely than in Kihoko, the hundred or so households of the *ekyaro,* or settlement area, of Kasingo. The air photograph facing page 1 in *Bunyoro* shows a part of this area. In the course of the year we were based there I got to know most of its inhabitants well and some of them very well, though not surprisingly I never acquired with them quite the same degree of mutual interdependence that I had achieved when living on my own in more remote Kihoko. Many of the people of Kasingo "commuted" to employment in Hoima daily, and since we were within easy cycling, and even walking, distance of the town, I later became a commuter myself, going into Hoima daily to interview people and to study official records.

I spent the greater part of the fourteen months from the beginning of August 1952 to the end of September 1953 at Kasingo. However I revisited Kihoko for several weeks during the year, and I also spent about two months working in a village near Masindi, in the north of the district. To begin with, as well as visiting and being visited by Kasingo neighbors, I spent a good deal of time reading government files at the district office and native court and other records at the headquarters of the Kingdom government at Hoima and at a number of chiefs' headquarters. At one time or another I visited most parts of the district to see specially influential people or promising informants. I also paid two or three visits to the East African Institute of Social Research at Kampala during this period, and took part in a conference held there in February 1953. I returned to Oxford in October 1953, but came back to Bunyoro for a further three months in the summer of 1955. Most of this latter period I spent in two villages on the Lake Albert shore, but I also revisited Kihoko and Kasingo.

In this chapter I consider the fieldwork methods I adopted under two broad heads: the use, first, of informants and assistants, and second, of documentary sources. In the next chapter I discuss the use I made of quantitative methods. I then briefly reconsider my relations with "authority" (in particular, with the district commissioner and the Bunyoro Kingdom government), and with such external agencies as the East African Institute of Social Research.

As I said earlier, I employed no full-time assistant or interpreter during my first six months in Bunyoro. On my second tour I did not engage one until after I had been back in the country for three and a half months, and then I employed only one. He was a young man with some secondary education who had been recommended to me by the Mukama, but unfortunately he did not take very much to the work, and this combined with some ill health made his attendance increasingly irregular, until at last he faded out altogether as an assistant, though we continued to meet at intervals. Not until April 1953, nearly nine months after my return to Bunyoro, did I succeed in engaging two satisfactory assistants, the younger of whom, a man of outstanding ability and intelligence and a natural ethnographer, died suddenly and tragically of meningitis less than three months later, whereupon his older colleague, who was apprehensive of sorcery, resigned. After a month's interval I then engaged another assistant, a very capable secondary schoolboy, for the last six weeks of my stay. When I returned in 1955 I had two competent assistants for the whole of my three months' visit.

Though not entirely my fault, my delay in recruiting adequate assistance was a mistake. If I were to have my time in Bunyoro over again, I should set about finding one, or preferably two, suitable men as a matter of urgency at the beginning of my second tour, that is, as soon as I had broken the ice and acquired a working, even if incomplete, knowledge of the language and culture. It may seem paradoxical to say that one works better without an assistant at the beginning of one's fieldwork; better with one after one has already accomplished the first and most difficult part of one's task. But it seemed plain to me then, as it still does, that a capable, English-speaking assistant-interpreter at the beginning would inevitably have slowed down rather than expedited the sometimes painful process of reaching terms of easy familiarity with the language and the people. Also, I realized that far better use can be made of an assistant-interpreter, with some knowledge of English, when one already knows the vernacular fairly well, for then difficult points of translation, obscure, archaic or elliptical phrases, and so on can be intelligently and profitably discussed. Unfortunately it was a little less clear to me that as soon as I could speak the language and knew fairly well what I wanted and how I should go about getting it, competent assistance could have doubled or trebled my intake of material.

The qualifications that I looked for in my assistants, whom I interviewed before appointing, were four. First, they had to have some secondary education; this meant that they had at least some understanding of English. Second, they had to be native Nyoro speakers, born and brought up in the country. Third, they had to be able to write Lunyoro fluently and well. Finally, and most importantly, they had to show a quick grasp of what I was trying to do, and a genuine interest in their own culture and in helping me to record it. This last qualification meant that, on the whole, younger men who had recently left school were the most suitable. The difficulty of course was that there were not at that time very many young men with these qualifications, and most of them were already employed. Also, the fact that they had been educated at mission schools (almost all education in Bunyoro was in the hands of the Christian missions) meant that they knew less about many aspects of their traditional culture than less highly educated boys with "pagan" backgrounds would have done; less even, in some matters, than I did. Most youths with secondary education had grown up in Christian homes; education had to be paid for, and few pagan parents saw much point in paying school fees for their sons once they had learned to read and write. Nevertheless, all of my assistants had grown up in rural environments and with some pagan neighbors and relatives, and their initial ignorance of and (sometimes) indifference to some aspects of their culture was a disability quickly remedied, once their interest was aroused.

I paid my ex-schoolboy assistants roughly what they would have earned if they had taken junior posts in government or business, or a little more; at that time around £6 (about seventeen dollars) a month. No doubt salaries have risen considerably since then. And I need hardly add that I treated them as friends and colleagues (which they were), rather than merely as paid employees.

The kinds of help that my assistants gave me covered most of the concerns that I discuss in the rest of this chapter and in the next. They acted as permanent informants, even though, as I remarked above, they often knew less to begin with about such aspects of Nyoro culture as sorcery, divination, and spirit mediumship than I did, from other informants and from the study of the native court records. But they very quickly learned. On such topics as kinship, marriage, and family life they provided clear and direct information from the start. They helped me in making sense of difficult texts, and in interviewing and "softening up" reluctant or suspicious informants. They recorded statements (texts) dictated by illiterate informants, and they wrote long accounts (case histories) of incidents in their own lives or that they had been told about. They assisted in house-to-house surveys, and they made use of their own ties of kinship and neighborhood to follow up promising clues and lines of inquiry. The best of my few assistants were not just clerks or interpreters but apprentice social anthropologists, and without them my work would have been very much poorer and more superficial than it is.

Interviews with informants were for the most part relatively unstructured (though of course I usually had a number of more or less specific questions in mind), except when I was seeking answers to questionnaires in the course of my household survey, discussed in Chapter 4. In the first period of fieldwork and in most of my "neighborhood" interviews later, my chief aim was to learn as much as I could about my informant himself and his position as neighbor and kinsman to others in the community. But as I learned more and began to pursue particular themes, such as land tenure, spirit mediumship, the role of chiefs, more knowledgeably, I began to seek out as informants people who had, or might be supposed to have, special knowledge in these fields. With them discussion tended to run deeply rather than broadly. Even so, it sometimes did range widely, and often important clues and insights would come from unexpected quarters. A discussion with a chief about land tenure, for example, might suddenly veer to sorcery, on which he might have unexpectedly valuable information. The wise field interviewer is indulgent of irrelevance and does not try to stick too closely to a preordained interview pattern. In fieldwork serendipity is a faculty not to be despised.

Bunyoro is socially highly stratified, and I interviewed a considerable variety of people at different levels in the hierarchy. I had several talks with the Mukama; though I owe much to his tolerance and help generally, he was not forthcoming as an informant. (Why indeed should he have been?) After one characteristically abortive visit, I reported in my diary as follows:

> In afternoon visited Mukama and gave him a present of Gordon's *Letters* and Stanley's *Through Darkest Africa,* which he had said he wanted before I went to England. He seemed pleased but did not *rongora* [*i.e.,* make a return gift]; instead he asked me who were the members of the English parliament in 1875, 1890, and 1952! I talked a bit about my work and my desire to meet Babito [members of the royal clan], etc., little if any response. . . .

My dealings with the king and my understanding of his ritual and political roles and of his complex palace organization were a major area of failure in my research. I say more about this later.

Other "important" local people whom I interviewed (as well as the local European administrators and missionaries) were many senior chiefs and members of the Mukama's government, down to the level of the village headmen, as well as several retired county chiefs (of whom there were a remarkably large number in the district), and Nyoro government officials, clergy, and teachers of all ranks. Clerks in both the district office and the Kingdom government headquarters were especially helpful; on many matters they are the best informed and most articulate members of the community. All of these officials, or most of them, are busy men, and it behooves the anthropologist to be grateful for the time and trouble they often willingly take to help him.

At the village or "community" level practically all of the anthropologist's neighbors are his informants at one time or another, but obviously some are more willing, knowledgeable and articulate than others. Thus one of my most useful informants in Kasingo combined the roles of both neighbor and district office clerk, and I obtained some of my best case histories from him. My nearest neighbor was the local village headman, a genial middle-aged man whom I came to know well, and I learned a great deal on informal visits to his house by just watching him dealing with some of the wide variety of matters for which lower-grade chiefs are responsible. I was impressed on several occasions by the combination of good humor, authority, and irritation with which he dealt with such matters as an urgent demand for laborers from the subcounty chief, for example, or an accusation of assault by one neighbor against another. Lower grade chiefs, in Bunyoro as elsewhere in Africa, performed exacting and full-time jobs for exiguous wages, with noteworthy intelligence, tact, and devotion. For the most part, also, with very little recognition; perhaps because the comprehensive and onerous nature of their duties was more clearly perceptible from the bottom than from the top.

After I had been in Kasingo for a few months I was visited by a neighbor who announced that he was a diviner, and that he was prepared, for a consideration, to divine for me, and to show me how it was done. Needless to say I accepted this offer with alacrity, and though I learned, at least to begin with, less than I had hoped, the fact that I was known to be in his confidence helped to open other doors. The fact that he later earned a gaol sentence for practising sorcery (not, I should add, through me) at least suggested that he was not pull-

ing my leg. Sometimes I traveled far afield to see people whom I had been told
might be specially well informed. Prisoners in the local gaol for such crimes as
sorcery or the practice of spirit mediumship were sometimes willing to talk
about such dangerous topics. Indeed, often they were much franker than other
people, presumably because they no longer had anything to lose by confession.
One middle-aged and unrepentant convict said to me in reply to my question
whether he would continue the practice of the *mbandwa* possession cult after he
was released: "Of course I will. *Mbandwa* bore me [a central emphasis in the
cult is on fertility], and I'm not going to give it up at my time of life, whether
they put me in prison or not!" My biggest coup was perhaps a series of interviews with a group of women converts to the revivalist and fundamentalist
branch of the Anglican mission called Balokole ("The Saved"), all of whom
had formerly practiced the proscribed *mbandwa* spirit mediumship cult, and
who were now perfectly happy to talk (again, of course, for a consideration)
about their activities as mediums. Their present state of grace may well have led
them to overstress the iniquities of their former way of life, but by making due
allowance for this, and by cross-checking the information they gave me with
other informants, I learned a good deal about the details of cult membership
and initiation.

This raises the question of payment to informants. There can, I think, be
no hard and fast rules about this; it depends on the culture one is working in,
and the value that the people themselves place upon their time and their knowledge. For most of the casual discussions with neighbors that made up the bulk
of my interviews the question of payment did not arise, though I was reasonably
lavish with cheap cigarettes, tea, and occasional beer parties. Nor did it arise in
regard to my interviews with senior chiefs and officials, and other eminent people. But when I had long discussions, sustained for several hours or even days
with people specially summoned to help me (as in the case of the Balokole la-
dies just referred to), I paid them a few shillings a day, to compensate them for
the time they had given up. For certain kinds of esoteric information, and for
the few demonstrations of divination and spirit possession (practices rigorously
proscribed by government and missions as "witchcraft") which I succeeded in
securing, I perforce paid quite substantial sums of up to twenty or thirty shillings or more. But such occasions were unfortunately rare. Again, I paid out
moderate sums of money as prizes for work submitted in response to my essay
competitions, which I describe below. As a general rule, however, I tried to convey to people that I was not there simply to buy information for my own private
(and mysterious) purposes; but rather that I was trying, with their help, to
learn as much as I could about their history, traditions, and culture, so that I
could write a book about them for the benefit both of people of other cultures who
might be interested and of later generations of Nyoro themselves. It is only to
be expected, however, at least in societies which have largely gone over to a cash
economy, that as people learn that their information is worth money they will
expect to be paid for it. I do not doubt that fieldwork in Bunyoro today would
cost more than it did in the fifties.

Observation, "Texts," and Official Records

Discussion of informants leads on to a consideration of the part played in fieldwork by observation and of some of the problems associated with it. For if what is observed is to make sense, especially in the early stages of fieldwork, it has to be explained to the foreign observer by informants. Of course one is observing, or at least one should be, from the moment one arrives in the country, and as one becomes increasingly accepted as a member, even if only an honorary one, of the community, one's observations become more and more "participant," for participation is a matter of degree. As a participant beer drinker I could and did observe people's public behavior at beer parties, and I was also an observer (though not usually an active participant) at such other public events as marriages, funerals, informal dispute settlements, court cases, and hunting and fishing expeditions. On such occasions my companions would generally tell me what was going on, and often I spent many profitable hours afterwards discussing the whole sequence of events in detail, either with one of my assistants who had accompanied me or with other knowledgeable informants.

But much goes on that one does not see, especially in Bunyoro where, as already noted, most houses are cut off from their neighbors by an impenetrable screen of bush and elephant grass. Also, the carrying out of most of the traditional ritual is of necessity secret, since to be detected performing it is to risk both legal and moral sanctions from government and missions. Further, Nyoro are a reticent people who lay great store by decorum and good manners, for which they have a special term, *makune*. It would have been unthinkable for me to have gone barging into people's houses uninvited, or to have intruded in their ceremonies or private parties without being asked. It is useful for an anthropologist to be thick-skinned, but not too thick-skinned, and any display of impatience, rudeness, or highhandedness would have cost me the hard-won confidence that I was gradually building up. In fact, as stated above, I did attend ceremonial and other social occasions, but always by invitation, either spontaneous or solicited, and rather less often, I think, than some other fieldworkers have done. I came gradually to realize that this "private" aspect of Nyoro social life would render me more dependent on a wide range of good quality informants than might otherwise have been necessary; this perhaps led me to an intensive if belated concern with acquiring the maximum amount of material in this way.

The obtaining of "texts," written statements either dictated by the informant to the anthropologist or his assistant and written down by him verbatim, or written down directly by the informant himself, is a vitally important part of modern fieldwork. For only by this means can the fieldworker record what the people themselves say about things, rather than merely what he says they say (or think) about them. Thus the culture is allowed, as it were, to speak for itself and, as we shall see in Chapter 4, such texts, with the anthropologist's commentary on them, form in due course an integral part of his published work. Texts can be about any topic whatsoever: what the informant thinks about his kinsmen, his neighbors, his rulers, the Europeans; birth, marriage, death, and the ceremonies associated with them; sorcery, divination, and spirit mediumship; fables, proverbs, or tribal history. Or they may recount actual events in the informant's personal life-story; the story of his marriage, of an occasion when he or a kinsman was the victim of sorcery and what was done about it, of a dispute to which he was a party, and so on. As well as being written down as texts by informants, such case histories may also be recorded by the anthropologist in his own words, either from his own observations (supplemented by information provided by participants), or simply from informants' accounts. I obtained a number of case histories by both of these methods, though by no means as many as I should have liked. Some of them have provided the central themes, or at least figured importantly, in a number of later publications. There are very brief examples on pages 68, 74, and 76 of *Bunyoro*.

But much of my most valuable textual material was submitted in response to two essay competitions that I organized during the year, with the help and cooperation of the Protectorate and Bunyoro Kingdom governments. The object of these competitions was to elicit material, not merely, nor even primarily, from schoolchildren, but from all literate Nyoro who might be interested. Inevitably much that was already familiar to me was sent in, and there was a good deal of repetition, but I nevertheless acquired a good deal of quite new information by this means. Many educated Nyoro competed; chiefs, clergymen, schoolteachers, clerks, as well as schoolboys and the barely literate, and some of the texts I received were remarkably informed and detailed. It seems that many Nyoro find it easier to write than to talk about the more esoteric aspects of their culture, and some of the essays I received, about sorcery and spirit mediumship in particular, as well as being valuable texts in their own right, opened up quite new vistas in these fields and suggested lines of inquiry which I profitably followed up later.

What I did was to prepare a circular letter, addressed to all county and subcounty chiefs, the heads of all missions and mission schools, and all government departments in the district, setting out the aims and terms of the competition. This was mimeographed and distributed through the courtesy of the district and local government offices. In the circular I explained briefly what I was doing in the country and on what kinds of topics in particular I wanted essays. I also said that prizes would be awarded—fifty shillings for the best, twenty-five shillings each for the two next best, and ten shillings each for the four next in merit. (These amounts would have to be considerably increased today to elicit a similar response). Here is a summary translation of the main points in my letter:

Customs of the Country

I think that some of you will know that I have come to this country in order to learn about the rules and customs of Bunyoro-Kitara, both those of long ago and those of today. When I have done this, I shall write a book which will explain about these laws and customs, both to people of other countries, and to your own grandchildren here in Bunyoro.

I cannot do this work properly without the help and advice of the people of Bunyoro. Where I have been staying many people have tried to help me and to explain things to me, but as I cannot go everywhere and see everyone in the kingdom, I have arranged a competition which will both help me in my work and provide some reward for those who enter for it.

This competition will encourage all of you who can do so to remember and write down things about your country. I know there are some very important Nyoro who know a great deal about the country and who have even written their own books about it, and I don't suppose they will want to enter; but if any of them would like to write to me and help me with their special knowledge I shall be most grateful to them.

The competition is like this: I want each competitor to write and explain about *one* of the topics listed below, as if he were explaining it to somebody who knew nothing about it. It doesn't matter how much you write; five pages, ten pages, or even more. These are the kinds of topics on which I would like people to write:

1. Different kinds of marriage.
2. Why women leave their husbands.
3. Birth.
4. Death and how it is dealt with.
5. Kinship.
6. Clans and subclans.
7. Sorcery and witchcraft.
8. Kinds of spirit mediumship.
9. Divination.
10. Cultivation.
11. Inheritance.
12. Personal names and their meaning.
13. Child rearing.
14. Proverbs and songs.
15. And any other matters of these kinds.

Competitors should remember that what is wanted is a full explanation of *one* of these topics, not just a few notes about several of them.

There followed details about the closing date for entries, the prizes, and the way in which the essays would be judged (by me, together with three senior Nyoro chiefs, one the author of a book on Nyoro history and tradition). There was also a hint that the authors of outstanding entries might, if they were interested, be offered employment by me as assistants.

It will be seen that I invited essays on a wide range of topics; themes which I knew to be important in Nyoro culture, and on which I needed more information. The residual category (item 15) was put in because I thought, rightly, that some candidates might wish to write on topics which, though no less interesting, I had not thought of. The emphasis on writing on one topic only was a very necessary one; despite it a number of entries consisted of just one or two superficial and worthless comments on a variety of themes.

This first effort produced some dozens of entries, some of which were of a very high standard indeed, especially on such esoteric topics as spirit mediumship, sorcery, and divination. The success of this first venture in systematically exploiting Nyoros' interest in their own culture led me to initiate a second competition six months later, towards the end of my second period of fieldwork. By this time my interests had narrowed and were a good deal less eclectic; I knew in which areas of my research I most needed information, and might hope to receive it. This time I therefore suggested only seven themes for the entrants to write about, and set out quite specifically the kind of information I wanted about them. However I again added a residual category. The following is a translation of these themes as I set them out in this second circular:

1. *Feasting.* Describe the various occasions on which people gather to eat and drink together. Give a full account of each such occasion. Describe fully everything that happened at a feast or feasts which you attended, and say how the people who were there were related to one another.

2. *Neighborhood and kinship.* Explain the advantages and obligations of neighborhood, and say how you personally behave as a neighbor. Also explain the advantages of being a member of a clan, with reference to your own experience. Are these privileges and obligations different now from what they were before the Europeans came?

3. *Good manners* (makune). Explain the different kinds of good manners, and the kinds of behavior that are approved of between different kinds of people. If these kinds of good manners have been "spoilt" since long ago, explain how this has happened.

4. *"In-law-ship"* (obuko) *and the mother's brother—sister's son relationship* (obwihwa). Explain the meanings of these terms. Particularly, does a father-in-law respect his son-in-law? Does a mother-in-law respect her son-in-law? Does a son-in-law respect his parents-in-law? Does he respect his siblings-in-law? And explain how a person's mother's brothers regard and treat him. Are they allowed to be angry with him?

5. *The state of the country.* Do you think that the people of Bunyoro are in a good state at the present time? If not, explain why you think that they are not.

6. *Neighborhood Courts.* What is a neighborhood court, and how can it penalize people? Explain the advantages of these courts, and the kind of people who take part in them. Describe particular cases you know about, and say exactly what happened.

7. *Sorcery.* Say all you know about sorcery and the different ways of practising it. Discuss, in particular, a particular case of sorcery which happened to you or to someone you know well, and what came of it: (a) were the sorcerer and his victim kin, and if so what was their relationship? (b) how was the sorcery diagnosed? (c) what was the reason for the sorcerer's attack, and how was it dealt with?

These themes reflected my developing understanding of Nyoro culture. Several of them related to categories of behavior or thought, or associations of ideas, that would not have occurred to me at the beginning of my fieldwork. They derive primarily from Nyoro ideas, not from my own. Thus "occasions for feasting" reflect a Nyoro categorization of social events. Nyoro constantly compare in-lawship and the mother's brother sister's son relationship; if they did not I should not have thought of doing so. "The state of the country" is frequently discussed by Nyoro, almost invariably to its disparagement, as it is by politically minded commoners everywhere. And the penalties imposed by neighborhood courts, informal fining in meat and beer, are not really "fines" at all, but at the same time both penalty and rehabilitation (*Bunyoro,* p. 69). All this confirms a point made earlier, that in an important sense it is the culture itself, as much as if not more than the anthropologist, that determines both what topics shall be investigated and the manner of their investigation.

This second competition was, if anything, even more successful than the first. Like it, it produced some thirty or forty entries, varying from a few scrawled pages to long and carefully worked out typewritten essays, the best of which were of very high quality. In my circular letter I had asked for illustrative factual material where possible, and many of the essays contained useful case histories.

In both competitions I and my fellow judges had little difficulty in reaching a unanimous decision as to the order of merit, and a list of the prize winners was given the same circulation as the original circulars. There were no complaints from unsuccessful candidates, and I later took on a prize winner in my first competition as a research assistant.

Where one is working with a literate or partly literate community and where one can count on the assistance or at least the tolerance of the local authorities (and of course many fieldworkers lack both of these advantages), this method of collecting information may be well worthwhile. It can even be carried on, if not quite so effectively, after the anthropologist has left the field. At the moment of writing I am attempting to launch a similar competition in Bunyoro (though for much enhanced prizes), with the object of acquiring material on folk tales, songs, proverbs, and traditional history. It is too early to say whether in the very different conditions of modern Bunyoro this venture will be as successful as my efforts more than a decade ago.

I now discuss the uses I made of existing written sources, accessible in Bunyoro during the time of my fieldwork there. (I do not consider here material published in books and articles, with most of which I was acquainted before I went to Bunyoro.) Such sources may be in the form of mission records, or in government files, returns, and the records of court proceedings. In Bunyoro little material seemed to be available from either of the missions (though I acknowledge that my enquiries about the possible existence of such material were less systematic than they should have been), perhaps because the derogatory view apparently taken of the Nyoro and their traditional culture by members of both missions was incompatible with any very serious interest in it. I should say here that the case is very much otherwise in many parts of Africa, where a great deal of invaluable ethnographic information has been recorded by missionaries, much (though happily not all) of which still lies unpublished in mission archives.

Through the courtesy of officials both of the Protectorate administration and of the Mukama's government, I was permitted to make considerable use of official records. As a former district officer in Tanganyika, my familiarity with the organization and working of government offices in East Africa was undoubtedly a help here. By these means I gained a great deal of valuable information on political affairs, the development of local government, and such matters, as well as much useful statistical and other information on demographic and economic aspects of Bunyoro. Equally, the files of the central office of the Bunyoro Kingdom government were a mine of important information, especially on postings, promotions, and transfers of present and former chiefs. I also made much use of the register of "rights of occupancy" held in the Bunyoro Kingdom government's land office, in connection especially with my enquiry into the working of Bunyoro's peculiar *kibanja* system of land tenure. Other government records of which I was permitted to make use were those of the district and coroner's courts, and the police files, the last two especially relevant to a study I later made of homicide and suicide cases in Bunyoro (Beattie 1960b). Outside Bunyoro I was allowed access to the central secretariat archives at Entebbe, where there was important material relating to the early days of British administration in Bunyoro.

But among the most valuable official sources for the social anthropologist in colonial and post-colonial Africa (this too I knew from my administrative days) are the written records of cases heard in the native courts. In Bunyoro such courts were held by both county and subcounty chiefs, and there was a central court both of first instance and of appeal, presided over by the Chief Justice (*Omuramuzi*) of the Bunyoro Kingdom government. A great part of the chiefs' time was taken up in court work, both civil and criminal. (Only some very grave offenses such as murder and rape and civil issues involving sums above a certain figure were dealt with in the district magistrate's court, and not in the native courts.) In Bunyoro these records were well kept, and although most of the criminal cases were concerned with breaches of various government regulations, some of them dealt with matters like sorcery and witchcraft accusations. They thus provided the means for making further breaches in the wall of secrecy that surrounded this side of Nyoro culture. Similarly, the civil cases heard in native courts provided much material on such topics as disputes arising from marriage, nonpayment or nonreturn of bridewealth, grounds of separation, and custody of children, as well as on cases of disputes over inheritance and debt. In addition, even though it has to be remembered that the native court system in Africa was in large part a British invention, the manner of conducting cases, the kinds of evidence admitted, the nature of the decisions reached, and the kinds of punishments awarded cast much light on Nyoro moral and legal norms.

I spent many hours poring over these records, both at the Kingdom government headquarters and in the various chiefdoms, and even so I left a vast amount of this invaluable material unanalyzed. But I did make a point of reading all the available records in the Central Court, and in those chiefs' and subchiefs' courts in whose areas lived the communities which I had studied intensively. My position as an investigator in these communities was obviously much strengthened when I learned, for example, from the court records that a man, whom I knew well and who had consistently denied that sorcery existed at all in modern Bunyoro, had recently been convicted and imprisoned for "being in possession of instruments of witchcraft."

4

The Second Tour: More Fieldwork Methods and Some Problems

Enumeration and Quantification

I NOW DISCUSS the uses I made of enumerative and quantitative methods. The first thing to stress is that I did not begin to use these methods until I had been in Bunyoro for twelve months and knew the language and the culture reasonably well. Obviously statistical information is worse than useless if the material that is being quantified is incompletely understood in the first place or, worse still, misunderstood. It was at least a year before I understood Nyoro social and cultural categories well enough to know what kinds of questions could most sensibly and usefully be asked about them. One context in which this is particularly important is when one is dealing with unfamiliar kinds of conjugal union. For often, as is the case in Bunyoro, there are several different types of union, all equally "legitimate," so that, for example, a simple division of unions into legitimate and illegitimate, depending on whether or not bridewealth has been paid, would wholly distort the realities of the situation. Further, where what is being quantitatively recorded has been misunderstood in its own social and cultural context, comparison with supposedly comparable (but really quite different) data from other cultures is likely to be hopelessly misleading.

I have never had any formal training in statistics (an omission that I regretted and still regret), so that my methods of acquiring and handling the data I used were no doubt somewhat naive and unsophisticated. But I do not think that this rendered either my mode of operation or my conclusions entirely worthless. In general, my aims were two. First, I wanted to provide a firm if not a completely adequate quantitative basis for the assertions about Nyoro society and culture that I felt increasingly justified in making as I got to know the country and the culture better: " many subcounty chiefs are directly appointed from outside the service and not promoted from the lower grades," "most

36

Nyoro marry neighbors," and so on. Nowadays it is not enough for the ethnographer simply to present his readers with unsubstantiated assertions of this kind; if they are to represent more than just his personal impressions he must adduce the quantitative evidence upon which they are based. Even if this evidence is a good deal less than perfect, being based perhaps on an insufficient range of evidence and on inadequate sampling techniques, it is a good deal better than no evidence at all.

My second and connected aim was to provide quantitative support for social and cultural correlations that had already suggested themselves to me as possible or even probable. Such putative correlations were, for example, between the payment of bridewealth and marriage stability, and between official chiefship and the proprietorship of a populated private estate (*kibanja*). In the first of these cases the quantitative survey strongly supported the view that at least in Bunyoro there was no clear correlation; in the second it strongly supported the view that there was. Quantitative analysis, however unsophisticated, may also suggest new correlations, which then call for investigation and explanation in qualitative terms. Thus, when I was investigating suicide in Bunyoro, it did not occur to me until I looked at my figures (exiguous though they were) that significantly more women than men committed suicide by hanging themselves at some distance from their homes, more men than women by hanging themselves in their houses; a correlation that I explained by reference to the greater degree of self-identification, in a patrilineal, virilocal society, of men than of women with their conjugal homes.

I used enumerative methods, based mostly on printed or mimeographed questionnaires, in four contexts particularly, in all of which I had a very clear idea of the kinds of information I wanted before I began. These contexts were, first, an enquiry into the career histories and social backgrounds of chiefs at all levels; second, an investigation into Bunyoro's curious system of land tenure, the *kibanja* system; third, a study in selected communities of modes of domestic grouping, household composition, incidence of marriage types, divorce, and so on; and fourth, a study of the incidence of and reasons for homicide and suicide. I consider these briefly in that order.

Though the changing role of chiefs in modern Africa had been one of my earliest anthropological interests, my study of Nyoro chiefs was largely inspired by the East African Institute of Social Research and its then director, Dr. Audrey Richards. She was at that time encouraging fieldworkers associated with the Institute to collect data regarding chiefs in a form that would make possible later comparison between the roles and career histories of chiefs in different areas of East Africa (this material was later published in Richards 1960). Individual fieldworkers were of course free to collect material in any way they liked, but in all areas information was sought on such matters as chiefs' education, religion, length of service, previous occupation, family background, and so forth.

I accordingly prepared a questionnaire form, which the Bunyoro Kingdom government office was kind enough to mimeograph and distribute for me. It asked each chief to provide information under the following heads:

1. Name, religion, place and date of birth.
2. Father's name, clan and occupation.
3. Names of agnatic relatives who were chiefs, palace officials, or held other important positions, with exact positions held.
4. Mother's clan, and names of matrilateral relatives who were chiefs, etc.
5. Wife's or wives' name(s) and clan(s). Names of affines who were chiefs, etc.
6. School(s) attended and standard reached.
7. Occupations since leaving school, present grade as chief, and length of time spent in it.
8. Is *kibanja* held? Number of certificate of occupancy.
9. Are you, or was your father, a "clan head" (*mukuru w'oruganda*)? If you are, when did you inherit this position?

This questionnaire was sent to all of Bunyoro's four county chiefs, twenty-five subcounty chiefs, seventy parish chiefs, and about 200 village headmen. Replies were received from all the county and subcounty chiefs, and from enough of the two lower grades of chiefs to make possible a reasonably comprehensive account of certain important aspects of contemporary Nyoro chiefship. Some of the information thus collected is in Chapter 4 of *Bunyoro* and, more fully, in Beattie 1960a.

My interest in the *kibanja* system of land tenure was stimulated early in my second tour by the district commissioner, for whom certain abuses of it were a matter of administrative concern. But I soon came to see that it was inextricably involved with the political system, so that neither could be adequately understood apart from the other. In the 1950s these *bibanja*, or populated private estates, which had formerly been a source of profit for their proprietors, had become rather a mark of prestige, and their "owners," whether they were salaried government chiefs or not, were popularly regarded as a kind of chiefs, with even more prestige than some official ones. Consequently as soon as an official chief was appointed he made a point of acquiring such a *kibanja*, unless he owned one already, in which case he would try to enlarge its boundaries. Most chiefs tended, however, to be somewhat reluctant to talk about their *kibanja* proprietorship, for the better educated of them at least knew that this assertion of "ownership" over proprietory estates and their peasant occupants was quite inconsistent with the existing regulations. I was therefore all the more grateful to the many chiefs who painstakingly completed a questionnaire form, again mimeographed and distributed by the courtesy of the local administration, seeking information about all *bibanja*, including their own, which were registered in the areas for which they were responsible.

The most important questions on the form were: the number and date of the certificate of occupancy; the name and clan of the first proprietor; his occupation when he acquired it; the name of the present proprietor (if different from the first); whether he had inherited it or "bought" it, and when; the number of households in the *kibanja* at the time when he acquired it and now. In the end I got information on some 369 tenanted *bibanja*, scattered fairly evenly through populated Bunyoro. This, together with the chiefs' career history forms, and of course notes deriving from my own observations and discussions, and the survey of a considerable number of *bibanja* on the ground, provided me with a reasonably comprehensive picture of the system as it existed at that time. There is some account of it on pages 37–39 of *Bunyoro,* and it is described rather more fully in Beattie 1954.

My house-to-house survey was very much the largest and most complicated of my exercises in quantification. For it I had (after useful discussion with and advice from the director and members of the East African Institute of Social Research) an enormous questionnaire form printed by the Uganda Bookshop in Kampala. This unwieldly document, which measured 22 inches by 12 inches, was perhaps the largest survey form ever used by a social scientist in East Africa, and I think now that I committed the common fault of the inexperienced and tried to fit too much into it. It was none the less useful, not only as a basis for statistical analysis, but also as a kind of *aide mémoire,* on which a considerable quantity of valuable information could usefully be stored.

It was designed so that one form should suffice for all but the very largest polygynous families, and was set out in eight horizontal sections. In the first section was entered the name of the household head and of all other persons normally resident in the homestead. Space was provided for entries in regard to each person under the following heads: sex, age, relationship to head of household, father's name, mother's name, clan, subclan, where born, religion, standard reached at school (if any), present occupation, former occupation(s), length of residence in this area, in this household, if now present, and if not, why not, and whither departed. The second section provided for the marital history of the (male) household head, space being provided for entries for wives up to six in number (if he had had more, a second form could be used). For each wife the following data were required: name, clan, residence before marriage, religion, educational standard, year of marriage to present husband, age at marriage, type of marital union ("ring"—*i.e.,* in a Christian church; with bridewealth; "free"; uxorilocal; or inherited), amount of bridewealth, if paid, in shillings and/or goats, whether still living with husband, or dead (if so, when?), or separated (if so, why?); and, if separated, whether the bridewealth (if paid) had been returned in whole, or in part, or not at all. The third section of the form provided for identical information in regard to the household head's wife's marital history, space being provided for details concerning up to six former husbands; if there were more than one woman in the household with previous marital histories, another form or forms could be used.

The fourth section provided a record of the children born to the women of the household (up to six), under two main heads: first, children born to the household head, and second, children born to other men (many married women had had children elsewhere). Under each of these heads provision was made for recording the following information, sexes being distinguished where appropriate: mother's name; number of miscarriages; number of children born alive, number still alive, number dead—of those who had died, number who died in infancy (under one year), later (over one year).

The remaining sections were less complex. The fifth provided space for information on the number and types of houses making up the homestead, whether these were of the traditional beehive type, rectangular, iron or grass roofed, and so on. The sixth section asked the household head to record the names of kinsmen living in the same and neighboring areas, and their relationship to him. The seventh covered the household's property—the number of cattle, sheep, and goats; whether a bicycle was owned by a member of the household; and the cash receipts in the previous year from the cash crops of cotton and tobacco (I neither expected nor achieved a very high degree of accuracy here). And the eighth and last section asked whether the household head owned a *kibanja* or lived on somebody else's; if the former, its registration number, the number of households and people resident on it, when and how it was acquired; if the latter, the proprietor's name.

The last four sections took up relatively little room and were on the reverse of the form, leaving most of that side of the paper blank. This I used for recording detailed genealogies for the household concerned, linking up its members, often by two or three different lines of connection, both with one another and with other members of the local community. These often quite complex genealogies enabled me to form a reasonably adequate picture of the genealogical structure of the local community; they were also useful in showing the degree to which links of kinship and affinity coincided with ties of neighborhood. I also recorded on the backs of the forms a good deal of other miscellaneous information relating to specific households and their members and a variety of general comments by informants on the various kinds of kinship and affinal relationships concerned.

During 1953 I used these forms, each of which took about an hour to complete, in carrying out house-to-house surveys in Kihoko (nearly two years after I had first settled there), in Kasingo, and Kisindizi, in the north of the district. In 1955 I carried out a further smaller survey in the village of Tonya on the Lake Albert shore. I received a good deal of help from my assistants, but I did most of the interviewing and recording myself. We covered, fairly completely, all the households in the three upland villages, forty-three in Kihoko, fifty-eight in Kasingo, and fourteen in Kisindizi. Only in one household, significantly that of a member of the aristocratic Bito clan, whose members have a not altogether merited reputation for haughtiness and arrogance, did I meet with outright refusal to cooperate, though in several other cases my powers of persuasion were severely extended. To compensate for taking up people's time and to enhance good will I paid an honorarium of one shilling to the head of every household interviewed.

I discuss in the next chapter how I dealt—and propose to deal—with the considerable body of information thus collected. Here I note only that the form was so designed that the data could be broken down under a number of broad heads, among the more important of which were household composition, and individual life and marital histories. The data could be regarded either from the point of view of the individual people concerned, or in reference to the marriages recorded, which could be considered as units in themselves. Adult individuals covered were 395 altogether (Kihoko 140; Kasingo 201; Kisindizi 54); individual marriages 389 (Kihoko 126; Kasingo 198; Kisindizi 65). Not the least important result of this somewhat arduous enterprise was the increased understanding of domestic life, and of kinship and neighbourhood relations, which I acquired in the course of carrying it out. After I had systematically visited every household in the area and had discussed with its members local as well as internal domestic affairs, often over a cup of tea or a glass of banana beer, I found that I had acquired a fairly comprehensive grasp of the essential features of family life and of village social organization.

The fourth context in which I made use of quantitative methods, this time on a very much smaller scale, was in a short study of homicide and suicide in Bunyoro, made in 1955 at the suggestion of Professor Paul Bohannan, who was then also briefly associated with the East African Institute of Social Research. In the summer of that year I examined in the district court, coroner's, and police files, by courtesy of the officials concerned, sixty-two case records of homicides and attempted homicides, and about the same number of suicide cases. These documentary researches were of course supplemented by enquiry into and detailed discussion of individual cases in the field, with people who had been in some way concerned with them or who had personal knowledge of them. Though the total numbers of cases about which I acquired adequate information were small, they did seem sufficient to warrant the drawing of a few general conclusions (Beattie 1960b; one such conclusion is referred to on page 37 above).

Note-Taking, Diary, and Photography

A few words must now be said about some of the more routine aspects of achieving and maintaining an adequate ethnographic record. I earlier described my method of note-taking: by the end of my first year in the field my filing system had been very largely reorganized; some heads had proved redundant and had been discarded, others had been subdivided, and a number of new ones had been made, to cover specific aspects of the culture that only emerged after I had been in Bunyoro for some months. Though I and my assistants made some use of notebooks, for the most part I recorded information, texts, and so on, on sheets of paper clipped *en bloc* to a board. When I could (and was not otherwise occupied or just too lazy) I typed out clean copies of my own scribbled notes in the evenings and filed them, making duplicate copies or cross-referencing when necessary. Some fieldworkers habitually make one or more copies of all their notes, as a precaution against loss; I did not do this, though no doubt there is much to be said for it. In any case, much of my material was written in longhand by my assistants or by literate informants, or transcribed from records, so that it would have been either redundant or unduly arduous to have made further copies of it. It is perhaps hardly necessary to add (though I caused myself much later inconvenience by neglecting this elementary rule in the beginning) that every note, however trivial, should be clearly inscribed with the informant's name (or other source) and the date.

I kept a diary, though not always very fully, during the whole period of my fieldwork. This is essential, even though it be used only to record such minimal data as one's movements in the area, one's more important visits and interviews, and major events in the community. If it contains a full record of the social and agricultural activities and interests of the community through a full agricultural year, so much the better. My diary record of the incidence of beer parties in Kihoko, for example, with notes of who were hosts and who guests on each occasion, showed how seasonal this form of entertainment is, as well as illuminating certain aspects of interpersonal relations in the area.

A diary may also serve as a useful safety valve when the frustations of which I spoke earlier crave some kind of expression; at all costs the wise anthropologist avoids venting them on the people who are his subject matter. The following extracts from my diary (not all dating from the early stages of my fieldwork) may serve to illustrate this point:

A very unsuccessful visit to ———, head of Basaigi clan, who was extremely suspicious, and put off by pert son of about 16. Wouldn't give account of anybody in his household [I was carrying out the last of the household surveys referred to earlier]; made all sorts of excuses—they weren't there and so he couldn't speak about them; I should ask the ow'omuruka [parish chief] for all the information I needed, etc. About 20–30 small children sitting and playing around, making a terrific din unchecked. Finally gave up and told him to talk to others and think about it. [I should add that I was more successful with him later.]

Feel rather browned off today altogether, and consider both ——— and ——— [my two assistants at that time, both excellent young men] practically useless and very tiresome. [I cannot now remember why!]

[Next day] A rather fruitless walk around the town [Tonya] in the morning, accompanied by ——— [a neighbor]. Conversations took usual form: "Nyowe ndi mukristayo, emizimu n'embandwa tizimanyire, ebi bye Shetani, oburogo tiburoho," etc. etc. ["I'm a Christian, I don't know anything about ghosts and spirits, these are things of the devil, there's no such thing as sorcery here, etc., etc."].

But such entries, and there are even less temperate ones, are the exception rather than the rule, though looked at years afterwards they provide a salutary reminder that fieldwork is not all the time a bed of roses. My diary record also enables me to recapture, after the lapse of more than a decade, something of the day-to-day vitality as well as the boredom of life in a rural African community; what Malinowski called the imponderabilia of ordinary life. It also, of course, enables me to present aspects of or stages in my fieldwork in their correct chronological order, when, as in certain parts of the present study, it is important to do so.

Photography is of course an important aid to ethnography, and though undistinguished as a photographer, I took a good many pictures, latterly mostly in the form of color transparencies, of the Nyoro scene and of Nyoro individuals. Where good professional photographs could be obtained, I did not hesitate to make use of them (with permission)—there are two in *Bunyoro*. I early realized how useful air photographs of the areas I had worked in intensively would be in plotting the dispersal of gardens and the pattern of settlement; making sketch-maps of settlement areas in Bunyoro on the ground, with its high grass and twisting paths, is a peculiarly tedious and time-consuming task. So early in my second tour I took advantage of a generous offer by Bunyoro's one remaining European farmer, who had a light aeroplane, to fly low over the Kihoko and Kasingo areas (to the considerable astonishment of their inhabitants), and to photograph their houses and fields through the open window of the plane. I obtained some interesting and informative pictures by this means, but their quality was a good deal less than adequate, and I later obtained some air photographs of professional quality through the kindness of an aerial survey firm at that time operating in western Uganda. One of them faces page 1 in *Bunyoro*.

I had no equipment for cinematography or sound recording: both, especially the latter (for the recording of oral texts, vocal and instrumental music, and such like) would have been invaluable, and I should certainly make some use of a recording machine at least if I were to go to the field now. But at the risk of being considered reactionary I would suggest that there are dangers in a too extensive reliance on mechanical gadgets which, apart from their tendency to go wrong, may all too easily come between the fieldworker and the individual people who are his real concern. Invaluable though these adjuncts are, they are no substitute for the close and sustained personal contact that is indispensable to good fieldwork in social anthropology.

Relations with Authorities

I now briefly review my relations, as a fieldworker, with the various authorities, both within and without Bunyoro, who were concerned in various ways with my research. I have already said something of my relations with Protectorate government officials, the Bunyoro Kingdom government, and the missions while I was in Bunyoro, and my indebtedness to the good will and help of members of all these organizations will be obvious from what I have written. Nowadays, of course, many of the "authorities," in Bunyoro as elsewhere in Africa, are different from those who wielded power a decade ago: political party officials, for example, and a new intelligentsia would have to be come to terms with, and often the place for an interview might be a club or a bar, as well as office or government headquarters. But an anthropologist who does not take pains to make himself agreeable and acceptable to the local authorities, whoever they are, and to explain to them as fully and as tactfully as he can what he is up to, may unwittingly cut himself off from access to much valuable material. At the same time, as I have explained, he must take care to avoid too close identification with "authority," with any ruling class or group, if he is not to prejudice his chances of acceptance at the peasant community level. This is certainly so in highly stratified societies like Bunyoro. The anthropologist must steer a middle course between the Scylla of a too complete identification with rulers and "government," and the Charybdis of disregarding or even antagonizing the "top" people, upon whose good will he may sooner or later depend. This is no easy task and may call for a high measure of tact and circumspection.

In the context of his relations with the local authorities, the question may arise how far, if at all, the anthropologist should respond to specific requests for information, or to suggestions that he should undertake research into matters of administrative concern. The answer, as so often, is that it depends. There is obviously no harm in giving administrators information on social or cultural matters when no confidence is breached or informant incriminated thereby, and I did so from time to time. But it would obviously be fatal to an anthropologist's research if he were to act or to appear to be acting as a government or mission spy. Again, if a piece of research requested by the government coincides or fits in with the anthropologist's own research programme, there is no reason why he should not undertake it and much is to be gained from the good will thereby engendered.

As already mentioned, my study of Nyoro land tenure was instigated in this way, though no doubt I should have pursued it anyway sooner or later. Early in my second tour the district commissioner expressed concern about the manner in which the *kibanja* system of land holding was apparently being exploited by the official chiefs and other important people, who were treating the certificates of occupancy (ostensibly granted only to peasant occupiers over the land which they lived on and cultivated) as titles to what were virtually populated freehold estates. He was also concerned with the question of how holders of occupancy rights over unpopulated areas scheduled for development should be dealt with.

I explained to him that I could not and would not advise on matters of policy that were purely of administrative concern, and pointed out that it would be quite impossible for me to go round overtly enquiring into such matters, as a kind of emissary of the district office. But I undertook to find out as opportunity offered what current attitudes and feelings about the *kibanja* system were (in Bunyoro as elsewhere in East Africa land tenure was a red-hot topic, and there was a widespread fear that the Europeans' real aim was to take the Africans' land from them), and how the system was actually being applied "on the ground." I eventually acquired a good deal of information on these topics, largely with the willing cooperation of the chiefs themselves, and eventually I was able to provide the district commissioner with a written report. This was grist to my mill as well as his, for I later wrote up this material as a conference paper for an East African Institute of Social Research Conference at Makerere (in February 1953), and afterwards as two articles (Beattie 1954). So as long as the anthropologist remembers that his first loyalty is to the people he is studying and whose trust he is trying to win, there is no reason why he should not show himself willing to help the administration, and indeed there are many good reasons why it may be to his interest to do so.

The position was very much the same in regard to the local government authorities, the Bunyoro Native—later Kingdom—government. But they, as

Nyoro, were more directly a part of my subject matter than the European administrators and missionaries were, at least as far as their cultural backgrounds
were concerned. It should be said parenthetically (and emphatically) here, however, that where, as was the case in much of Africa during the "colonial inter-
lude," Europeans play a significant part in the social and political systems of the
peoples social anthropologists study, the roles they do play should be fully and
systematically investigated, for they form an important part of the whole net-
work of social relations which is the anthropologist's central concern. It will be
very plain from what I have already said how much I owed to the help and
good will of local government officials and chiefs at all levels. I took pains to
establish and maintain, as far as I could, good relations with all of them—with
some I achieved genuine friendship. I referred earlier to the real regard that I
acquired for these men, many of whom carried out difficult and exacting tasks
for very low salaries, with noteworthy skill, devotion, and intelligence.

I have already mentioned my relations with the missions, and from members of the Church Missionary Society (the Native Anglican Church) in particular my wife and I enjoyed both help and hospitality. Some of its native clergy
were valuable informants. But as my fieldwork progressed I could not help feeling that the uncompromising stand taken by many missionaries against such traditional institutions as polygyny, and more particularly against the traditional
ritual and religious cults, not all of which could be said to be morally objection-
able by Western Christian standards, though some could, in some ways did more
harm than good. It certainly did not make my work any easier. Two further short
extracts from my diary may express something of the frustration thus engendered:

> [At Kaiso, in the Lake Albert rift valley] After all this [a long and often-
> repeated speech about myself, my neutrality, and my good intentions] the
> response to an enquiry about, e.g., a spirit hut is: "Oh, it's just something
> we put there for the children to play in (!). Or, "We don't know anything
> about these things, our grandfathers did but they're all dead now, and we
> realize that they were misled by Satan." Or, "We don't have any *embandwa*
> (spirit cult) in Kaiso now" (!! in fact they have one for practically every
> house!); "if our wives don't have children we send them to Hoima to be
> examined by the doctor," etc.

> This is all a bit frustrating.

A few days later.

> One informant said that ——— [a local missionary] castigated *ebikondo*
> [ancestral shrines], like all other ritual things, as of *Shetani* and "witch-
> craft." He naturally resented this, as all Banyoro, at least those who are not
> too cowed to resent anything, do.

> I have been, almost involuntarily, acting as a strong anti-mission influence
> here and at Tonya. *Why* force people to give up their traditional cults,
> which do no harm and satisfy spiritual needs, and compel them to adopt
> an alien religion? Polygyny is another stumbling block: why shouldn't a
> man have two wives? [I should, in a cooler moment, have added "in the
> conditions of pagan and preliterate Bunyoro"]. Why not desecrate mosques

and execrate Moslems? Gentle persuasion and preaching would perhaps be tolerable, but compulsion and bullying and coercion in these matters are not.

But despite these outbursts, I had, and have, nothing but admiration for the dedicated and devoted work done by missions of all denominations in Bunyoro and elsewhere, and for the many individual missionaries whom I know and respect.

Outside the Bunyoro district, the most important influence during my period of fieldwork was the East African Institute of Social Research at Makerere, with which I was informally associated during most of my time in Bunyoro, and its director and fellows. I visited Kampala several times during my fieldwork, and I took part in two of the Institute's conferences. As I have already acknowledged, I derived much stimulus from its director, Dr. Audrey Richards, and I was always conscious of my good fortune in having a center of fellow social anthropologists and other social scientists only a day's journey away.

Outside East Africa I retained vital contact, of course, with the Institute of Social Anthropology at Oxford University where I was registered as a doctoral student, and especially with my academic supervisor there, Dr. John Peristiany, and the head of the Institute, Professor Evans-Pritchard. Though not the best of correspondents, I maintained touch with these teachers, and with several of my fellow students, throughout my fieldwork. The Treasury Committee for Studentships in Foreign Languages and Cultures, who financed my fieldwork, were both generous and unexacting. In addition to some account of my expenditure, they required two-monthly reports on the progress of my research, and although I was sometimes dilatory I kept the Committee reasonably *au fait* with the development of my work. I found that the necessity to reflect at two-monthly intervals on what I had been doing and what I planned to do was by no means a waste of time.

Assessment

What, at the end of my fieldwork, did I consider to be my most important achievements and failures in the field? When I left Bunyoro in October 1953 to take up my present post at Oxford, I still had more than a year of my Treasury grant to run, but I felt, partly because I was rather older than most research students, that I would be unwise to let pass the opportunity of so congenial a post. Nevertheless I knew that my fieldwork was woefully incomplete, and I felt that I had only just begun to break through to a deeper understanding of Nyoro society and culture. But I knew, too, that however long his stay in the field no one ever thinks his fieldwork complete, and of course it never is. Besides, I hoped that I should have the opportunity to return to Bunyoro later, to repair some of its deficiencies. I did indeed have such an opportunity in 1955, and I made, I think, full use of it. But fieldwork, at the stage that I had reached towards the end of 1953, depends largely on a wide and shifting range of sometimes tenuous personal contacts, and even after the lapse of two years it is difficult, even impossible, to pick up all the threads again.

None the less there was a fair amount, I thought, though without complacency, on the credit side. I could speak Lunyoro with reasonable fluency. I understood, I believed, the essentials of Nyoro kinship terminology, and the values and usages associated with it. I knew what were the more important values of community and neighborhood, and I understood pretty well how the political system worked, as a complex of interlocking roles and statuses reflecting both traditional and Western standards, and what people thought of it. I had learned, mostly through texts and long discussions with informants, a good deal about the ritual side of Nyoro culture, of which, to begin with, I had despaired of ever learning anything. I had a suitcase full of files containing, I hoped (only too correctly!), enough material in the shape of notes, texts, and figures to occupy me for years. I believed that I could, in due course, present a reasonably adequate picture of most aspects of Nyoro social and cultural life, despite serious *lacunae,* of which I was only too well aware.

Some of these I have already referred to. The gravest was undoubtedly my failure to make a thorough study of the contemporary organization, both social and ceremonial, of the Mukama's palace, and of his extensive regalia. I obtained a good deal of information about palace affairs from informants who either had at one time worked there (thus an ex-private secretary of the Mukama was a mine of information) or who had relatives who did work or had worked there. But I never had the opportunity to visit the palace informally or to interview *in situ* its numerous staff of officials and retainers. As I noted earlier, the Mukama's responses to my occasional suggestions that he might, at his convenience, show me around the palace and explain to me something of the significance and history of his extensive regalia were negative.

I think that there were two main reasons for this. The first I have already referred to. It was that by electing to start my researches in the "bush" and not at the capital I was bound, despite my explanations and justifications, to perturb and in some measure to alienate some important figures at the center. And the second was that by the time I came to work at Hoima, in my second tour, I had heard a good deal of grumbling from various sources about the Mukama and his government, and had collected much information about such matters as the circumstances in which particular chiefs had been appointed, transferred, and promoted, matters which at that time were practically entirely in the Mukama's hands, and were sometimes dealt with in terms of traditional, rather than modern, bureaucratic norms. The fact that I had acquired information of this kind was of course known to the Mukama and his personal advisers (though I was as discreet as I could be), so it was perhaps not altogether surprising that they were not overwhelmingly eager to give me free access to the palace and its inner workings.

So a detailed study of the royal palace of Bunyoro, its history, organization, and, especially, a full account of its regalia still remains to be carried out. But if it ever is made, it will, I believe, have to be by an African. It would be best of all if it were carried out by a Nyoro and a Mubito, himself a member of the royal family or closely connected with it, and with training in social anthropology. Unfortunately I know, as yet, of no likely candidates for this task. I do not believe that it can ever be carried out by a Western anthropologist, though I may be mistaken.

The next major area in which I should have liked to push my fieldwork further was in the study of ritual, especially of the ubiquitous Nyoro spirit mediumship cults. Certain dimensions of ritual behavior are naturally not open to observation in most societies; one does not, for example normally hope to witness sorcerers in action. But the wall of secrecy that surrounded all forms of traditional ritual behavior in Bunyoro was exceptional. It was also entirely comprehensible in view of the rigorous and undiscriminating repression to which all traditional cults had been subjected for more than half a century. This had not had the effect of eliminating these cults, indeed some of them had proliferated in recent years. But it meant that not until the last months of my fieldwork was I allowed to witness either techniques of divination or a ceremony of spirit mediumship, and the latter had been specially arranged for my benefit and so was hardly typical. I believe, though I may be deceiving myself, that when I left I was on the verge of a breakthrough here. Among other projects, I had just concluded an agreement with a friend of mine, who had been advised to become an initiate in a spirit medium cult, that I should pay his expenses (which were considerable) on condition that I was allowed to witness all or most of the proceedings, but unfortunately I had to leave Bunyoro before they could take place. Also, people were rapidly becoming much less reticent on these matters, as my knowledge grew. But it is idle to speculate on what might have been. I was fortunate to have gained a good deal of material from informants, largely in the form of texts and case histories, of which most has now been published. I was also fortunate, and this point can hardly be overstressed, to have worked in a society of rapidly advancing literacy (obviously no essay competition could be held in a preliterate community), and also one in which, in the twilight of colonial rule, ready co-operation could be looked for from both central and local governments.

This brings me to a third area of research in which, if I were undertaking my study again, I should do more than I did. This is the field of tribal and clan histories, of myth and legend, and of stories, songs, proverbs, and riddles. I did do some work on some of these themes, but I felt, as many of my contemporaries did at that time, that in the limited period available higher priority attached to such more "structural" concerns as kinship, political organization, dispute settlement procedures, and such like. The importance of such nonstructural, "literary" material has come into the forefront again in recent years, with the increasing recognition that not only is it often of high literary and esthetic merit in its own right, but also that it often conveys unique insight into the social and cultural categories and values of the people who have it. Were I to have my time in Bunyoro over again, I would have invited more such material in my two essay competitions, and I would also (had I been able to afford it) have employed one or more assistants just to record texts of these kinds. I should add in parenthesis that I am now trying to make up for lost time by initiating, at long range and with the help of the new Runyoro-Rutooro Language and Literature Committee in Uganda, a new competition, in which competitors are to be invited to submit essays on such "literary" themes. It remains to be seen whether it is too late.

In the end, my regrets are the regrets of all fieldworkers, that I did not get more material than I did. The essential thing is to record as much as possible, in the form of one's own notes, texts written or dictated by others, case histories, and archival material. Although, after a decade, I have not yet finished processing my own records, I should still be glad to have much more such material than I have. I could, perhaps, have got it, even in the time that I was in Bunyoro, if I had engaged adequate literate assistants, preferably (if I had then been able to afford them) more than two, a few months earlier than I did. But whether, in the circumstances of my research in Bunyoro in the early 50s, with limited resources, I could have done a very great deal more than I did do is a question that I am content to leave unanswered.

5

"Writing Up" and Conclusions

Stages in Written Presentation

SOME ANTHROPOLOGISTS find the labor of preparing the results of their field-work either for presentation as a thesis for an advanced degree or for publication in article or monograph form by far the most difficult part of their task. And indeed, if a young fieldworker moves straight from the field into a teaching post, as I did, he will find that at least for several months or even years practically all of his time is taken up in writing new lecture courses, and in preparing for and participating in classes and tutorials. But pleasant though it may be to be able to sit down in study or library for a year or so, and to prepare one's material for publication without interruption, it *can* be written up in bits and pieces, as opportunity offers, though of course it takes longer. In fact, the stimulus of teaching, and the necessity it entails of expressing oneself clearly, may sometimes bring the anthropologist to a better grasp of some of his own field problems. And if any part of his teaching is based on his field material, the process of preparing it as lectures also forms part of the process of preparing it for publication. After I returned from Bunyoro I gave courses of lectures on such themes as Nyoro kinship and affinity, Nyoro political institutions, and Nyoro ritual before publishing on these topics. My notes for these lectures, after polishing and discussion with colleagues and students, formed the first early drafts of what later became chapters in my doctoral thesis, and, at a still later stage, articles in journals and symposia, and (in condensed form) chapters in *Bunyoro*.

There is an important sense in which writing up is a continuous process with fieldwork itself, especially if one adopts the method I used, however unsystematically, for recording material in the field. For by filing one's notes and records under the appropriate headings as one collects them, specific subject files are gradually built up and these may sometimes provide a basis for systematically interconnected studies of particular themes and therefore later for an article or a series of articles on these themes. Thus "writing up" is very much a matter of degree, and some anthropologists will in fact already have done some writing while still in the field. If a fieldworker can have a break in the middle of his tour, as I had (and I think that, if possible, all fieldworkers should), he is well advised to spend at least some of it in writing an account of his findings to date. This will enable him both to determine where he stands in regard to his research and how far he has got, and to plan the lines on which to develop his future work in the field. It will also provide a basis for profitable discussion with his supervisor, teachers, and fellow students. The task of preparing a 10,000 word report for the Treasury Committee in 1952 was of great value to me in this way; as also was the writing of the paper on Nyoro land tenure, referred to earlier, which I prepared in the field some months later and read to a conference at the East African Institute in 1953.

There may be said to be four stages in the process of writing up one's field material; at least this was so in my case. Though these stages may overlap and even, sometimes, change their order, and though one may have reached one stage with some parts of one's material and a different stage with other parts, they do conveniently if somewhat arbitrarily distinguish four separate levels in the "processing" of one's data. The first stage is the initial presentation of one's material in the form of talks, seminar papers, and lecture courses. The second is the submission of all or a large part of it as a doctoral dissertation or thesis. The third is its presentation piecemeal as published notes or articles, or as contributions to symposia on selected themes, and the fourth its final publication in the form of full-length books or monographs. I now briefly consider each of these four stages, with particular reference to my own work.

As soon as a social anthropologist returns from the field, even if he is not at once involved in the preparation of lecture courses, he is likely to be invited from time to time to give talks both in his own university department and elsewhere. This provides an excellent incentive for him to begin to get his material, or some parts of it, into intelligible and publishable shape. If he is at the same time engaged in preparing lectures based on his ethnography, this too can obviously be combined with the longer-term interests of thesis and publication. From 1953 onwards I gave talks from time to time at Oxford and elsewhere on particular aspects of Nyoro culture, and, as I noted above, some of my earliest lecture courses were on my field data. These preliminary efforts to organize and present my findings, and the discussions of them that my talks and lectures sometimes evoked, were an important stage in the progress of my own writing.

My doctoral thesis, entitled *The Banyoro: a Social Study of an Interlacustrine Bantu People,* was my first attempt to present the main body of my material as a systematic whole. This I did, broadly, in terms of what I had come to see as the two main category distinctions or dualisms in Nyoro social structure, the distinction between the superimposed state or kingship (*obukama*) and the village community on the one hand, and the ubiquitous superordination-subordination theme on the other. Thus in the first part of the thesis I dealt with the king, his chiefs, and the centralized system of authority structured around them; in the second part I dealt, rather more superficially because the field was more diffuse, with the various relationships and values centering on neighborhood and kinship. This pattern was, I believe, dictated to me rather by the nature of Nyoro society and culture themselves than by my own interests and predilections, though no doubt these played a part too. It is reflected in the design of *Bunyoro: An African Kingdom*.

To the question whether one should regard one's thesis as potentially a book and seek publication of it either as soon as it has been examined or after some revision and modification, different anthropologists have given different answers. Some, in fact, have rushed straight into full-length publication with an ethnographic monograph as their first published work. But my answer to this question was a fairly categorical "no." (I should in fairness add that I was not conscious of any very intense pressure to publish my thesis as a book from those who had read it!) It seemed to me that my thesis, as a first attempt to present a coherent picture of Nyoro society and culture, required a good deal more thinking about and revision before final publication. For this reason among others, I decided to aim at the initial publication of my material in the form of relatively brief articles on specific themes, rather than as a comprehensive monograph.

There are, it seemed to me (and still does), several important advantages in going through this third stage in the process of preparing one's field material for final publication. The first and most practical one is that since it does not take so long to write an article as to write a book, a young anthropologist can hope to achieve a reasonable amount of published work in a comparatively short time, despite the heavy pressures of teaching and supervision to which he is likely to be subjected during his first years in an academic post. A second consideration, of more importance in its bearing on the quality of the author's work as finally presented, is that ethnographic material thus published piecemeal can benefit from the comment and criticism of colleagues and other interested scholars before it assumes final shape in monograph form. Further, the writer allows himself longer to think about his own material; thus he will be able to place it more surely in the contexts of his other findings and conclusions about the same culture, of current theoretical interests in the subject, and of comparable ethnographic material from elsewhere. (This last point is particularly important, for the anthropologist who is insufficiently acquainted with comparative ethnography is likely to use "his" people as a yardstick for all anthropological problems everywhere.) At the same time he will avoid unduly delaying its preliminary publication. An anthropologist who has completed a spell of fieldwork has always to keep in mind the obligation he is under to his fellow anthropologists, to the university or foundation that supported him, and, nowadays, to the people whose culture he has studied (as well as, of course, to himself) to communicate to others as quickly as he can something of what he has been paid to find out. A scholar with no teaching commitments may have time and opportunity to present his findings in full-length books without delay. But the anthropologist who can only do his writing in the intervals of teaching is well advised to consider the advantages of initial publication in article form.

If he is wise, however, he will have constantly in mind the ultimate presentation of his material in a full-scale monograph or monographs, and as he

proceeds with his writing the design of these works will in all probability gradually take shape in his thinking. Thus the score or so of papers that I have published about Bunyoro since I completed my second tour of fieldwork (I am still
adding to them slowly) are a long way from covering all of my ethnographic
findings, but it has become increasingly clear to me as I have worked on them
that they fall into three broad categories, though naturally there is some measure
of overlapping. First, there are those papers relating to the Nyoro kingship, the
chiefs, the land-tenure system, dynastic history, and the realm of political activity
generally that, together with as yet unpublished data in this field, fall conveniently under the heading of the Nyoro State. Second, there are articles on kinship and
affinity, on dispute settlement at village level, together with much unpublished
material on marriage and divorce, on types of village settlement, neighborhood,
and so on, that fall equally clearly under the heading of the Nyoro Community.
And finally, I have published a dozen or so articles on aspects of the complex of
Nyoro magical and religious practices and beliefs, material which might appropriately from the content of a monograph on Nyoro Ritual. I hope, therefore,
in due course to publish three full-length monographs with the above titles, but
even if, as is only too likely, this project is greatly delayed or only partly
achieved, or even if it is never achieved at all, at least some part of the material is
on permanent record in the shape of articles and contributions to symposia. At
the end of this book I have included a list (it is a very short one) of my writings
to date, mostly in the form of brief articles, about Bunyoro, under these three
heads. Immodest though this premature exercise in bibliography is, it does, I
think, convey some idea of the manner in which the apparently haphazard publication of ethnographic articles over a period of years may gradually come to assume a clear and integrated pattern.

Thus the third stage of publication runs, or should run, into the fourth, the
preparation of a full-scale monograph or monographs on one's fieldwork. I hope
I have made it plain that these various stages are by no means separate or self-
contained; work may and often does proceed on all levels at once. As in the field,
so in writing up, the anthropologist is likely to have many irons in the fire simul-
taneously. So far the only book I have published on my fieldwork is the case
study *Bunyoro: An African Kingdom,* and I did this mainly on the lines of my
doctoral thesis but more concisely and with many omissions and simplifications,
contemporaneously with writing on other levels and on other topics. But any
clarity and organization the book possesses are due to the fact that I had time to
think about and to assimilate thoroughly the field data upon which it is based,
first by presenting them as a doctoral thesis, and then, in regard to some of the
material at least, in the form of brief articles on specific themes.

One area of "writing up" in which I have been particularly dilatory is in
the processing of the quantitative data, mainly relating to domestic grouping,
marital histories, and the like, which I collected in the course of the village surveys that I carried out in 1953. However I took advantage of the facilities gener-
ously afforded by the Center for Advanced Study in the Behavioral Sciences at
Stanford, California, when I was a fellow there in 1960, to codify all the materi-

al I had collected on my survey forms and to have it committed to IBM cards. I had two sets of cards punched: one relating to the statuses, life histories, and marriages of 395 adult individuals; the second covering 389 marriages, in terms of the type of union, and of such matters as the ages, education, religion, and previous marital histories of the spouses. I have not yet found time or opportunity to work systematically through this considerable body of data (the "adult individual" cards, for example, provided for entries under fifty separate heads). My failure to do this may be partly due, also, to an innate resistance to—and incapacity for—quantitative analysis. But at least the material, even if not so far published, has been committed to intelligible and enduring form. It will, or should, form an indispensable part of my second projected monograph, on the Nyoro Community.

In general, I have found the central problems of writing up are closely correlated with the central problems of fieldwork itself. They are, first, how best to represent the facts of the society and culture studied, what people do; and second, how to communicate an adequate representation of what people *think,* how they comprehend and categorize their social and cultural universe, how the world they live in looks to them. The first problem requires, in written presentation as well as in understanding in the field, case histories and the intelligent use of quantitative methods. The second requires the publication of texts, as they were written or spoken by members of the society themselves, either in translation or (ideally) in the vernacular, with appended translation, comment, and analysis. The day of impressionistic, anecdotal anthropology is past, and no report on a field study can nowadays be taken seriously unless it provides both a quantitative account of the facts of observed social behavior, and a qualitative account of the culture, supported by adequate textual material. By this latter means the field data are brought back into the study and made available, as it were, raw and not predigested for other scholars.

This second task, that of communicating not just an account of behavior but a comprehensive and meaningful picture of the ideas, values, and beliefs of members of another culture, is perhaps the most difficult; it is certainly not the less important. Translation even from a quite closely related language is notoriously difficult (translation from French to English, for example, constantly raises almost insoluble problems), but translation from a language wholly alien in structure and thought raises these problems very much more constantly and acutely. Thus, in this sphere, the process of writing up becomes a kind of conceptual exegesis; a term in the language of the culture studied may cover a range of meanings so unfamiliar in the anthropologist's own culture that there is not even an approximately appropriate term by which to translate it in his own language. So he has to write a detailed exposition of the various significances and usages that the term has in its proper culture, and this can only be done if he understands that culture intimately and in detail. This was the procedure I attempted to adopt in dealing, for example, with the characteristic and untranslatable Nyoro concept of *mahano* (Beattie 1960c). Modern ethnographic writing is increasingly concerning itself with semantic problems of this kind.

The Fieldworker and Moral Responsibility, and Concluding Remarks

I conclude with a few words about two major themes, both of which have been touched upon in earlier chapters. The first is the question of the degree to which the anthropologist becomes, or may become, involved with the people he studies. And the second is the broader question of what, in the end, fieldwork is really about; what is the point of it all?

It is plain from what has already been said that it is impossible for the social anthropologist, living and working in close contact with the community he is studying, not to become involved in some degree with his neighbors, as friends and fellow humans. In so far as he regards them as people, and not merely as actual or potential informants, he is bound, in the Kantian phrase, to treat them as ends in themselves, and not as means only. Thus, like other anthropologists, I dealt with people's minor ailments, conveyed them to a dispensary or hospital, made them temporary cash loans, and so on. I did these things not simply because I calculated that I would in the end get more information from them by doing so (a doubtful proposition anyway), but rather because it would have been inhuman not to.

Anthropologists have sometimes written as though all that need be considered is the effect of fieldwork on the fieldworker himself; much less attention has been given to its effects on the people studied (Barnes 1963 is a notable exception). But, consciously or unconsciously, the anthropologist is affecting the people he is working with all the time. Obviously no responsible anthropologist will betray to the authorities the fact, say, that a neighbor has been distilling illicit liquor, or has successfully evaded a tax obligation. But it is very much a matter of degree. When I learned, for example, that a respected neighbor, employed in the local hospital, was stealing syringes and giving injections with an unsterilized needle to local people for a fee, I felt justified in suggesting to the medical authorities that increased vigilance might be desirable (and in attempting to persuade the amateur physician of the importance of asepsis). But I did not feel justified in reporting the matter to the police. The anthropologist who learns a good deal about his neighbors in confidence must respect that confidence, except for overwhelming reasons, though it is of course conceivable that there might be occasions when he should not. No hard and fast rules can be laid down; these are matters of conscience rather than of science.

But the anthropologist's effect on the people he studies may be more insidious. Thus there may be real danger from his own community for the informant who is persuaded, for cash or otherwise, to divulge secret information about esoteric aspects of his culture, such as cult initiation or sorcery techniques. I told in Chapter 3 how after the death of one of my informants from meningitis his colleague resigned, fearing sorcery. I was, some years later, rather shaken when I heard rumors of the death of another young man who had been for a short time my companion and informant on a visit to the Lake Albert villages, and who had given me a good deal of information about the spirit cult in that area. I have no grounds for supposing that his death (if it occurred) was not a natural one, but it is widely believed that *mbandwa* mediums can kill by sorcery those who betray their secrets, and I do not doubt that there are men in most Nyoro communities who have a knowledge of poison (itself a branch of *oburogo*, "sorcery") and who sometimes make use of this knowledge. All that the anthropologist can do is to exercise tact, common sense, and consideration, and not to be too exigent in his demands for esoteric information from reluctant informants. He should remember that fieldwork is a two-way process.

Increasingly, also, the question arises how far and in what form confidential information should be published (this question is also well discussed in Barnes 1963). As the anthropologist increasingly studies communities that are either already literate or are rapidly becoming so, the probability increases that his work will be read by at least some of the subjects of it. Here again, the anthropologist must use his discretion, bearing in mind not only the risk of being served with a writ for libel, and the possibility that he or another sociological investigator may some day wish to return to that community, but also the pain or embarrassment he may thereby cause to his erstwhile neighbors and companions. At the present stage, at least for workers in rural or tribal areas, the people they write about are usually sufficiently protected by such devices as changing the names of people and places. This is not so, of course, where a readily indentifiable person such as a ruler or chief is being discussed, and here great discretion may be necessary. Again, no simple solution can be offered, but it is certain that this problem will become increasingly acute.

Most (though not all) anthropologists develop a real affection for the people among whom they have spent a year or more of their lives, and they may, for this reason, find themselves playing on their account some small part, formally or informally, in larger affairs. They may, for example, even long after they have left the field, feel themselves bound to protest against some injustice or discrimination, or to register their support for some project or movement for that people's benefit. Thus in 1962, when the immediate return to Bunyoro of the "Lost Counties" (see *Bunyoro*, pp. 22–23) was recommended by two Royal Commissions, I felt impelled to write letters to the British national press, and to prepare a memorandum for distribution to members of Parliament and others concerned, representing Bunyoro's case as forcefully as I could. Though, at least while he is in the field, neutrality and noninterference are two of the anthropologist's most necessary qualities, other anthropologists have at one time or another become similarly involved in the affairs of the peoples they have studied. Here again, involvement is a matter of degree. The important thing is that anthropologists should remember that whether or not they take overt action in matters concerning the community they have worked with, it is certain that they cannot avoid affecting the members of that community in some degree and in a variety of ways.

I turn now to my final question: What, in the last resort, is fieldwork about? For the social anthropologist there is a short answer. Fieldwork is an attempt to understand, by close and direct contact, how a living community works, and what are the beliefs, norms and values by which it lives. The fieldworker's findings, when presented in the context both of comparative ethnography and of current research interests and problems in social anthropology, provide the indispensable raw material for theoretical advance in the subject. But fieldwork is more than simply an attempt to answer, by the use of questionnaires, survey techniques, and the like, specific questions on specific themes, economic, political, or whatever (though, as we have seen, there can be no fieldwork without specific questions): it is rather an attempt to comprehend the whole way of life of that community in the round. Still less is it an attempt by questioning aged informants and analyzing tradition and myth, to reconstruct some putative earlier condition of the society, uncontaminated by foreign influence. Though here again, when history and myth are relevant to present-day concerns (as they almost always are and certainly were in Bunyoro) they will naturally fall within the social anthropologist's sphere of interest.

But essentially the fieldworker is interested in the present, in the actual human community that he sees moving, talking, living around him. At least in the context of most African societies, this means that he is essentially concerned with the consequences of social change and of the contact of cultures. An anthropologist who describes a modern African society as though it had not been extensively and radically affected over a period of many years and at all levels by the impact of European governments and missions and, often, of farmers and traders, is misrepresenting what he sees. Almost every aspect of Nyoro culture had been affected by Western influence, so that, in the nature of the case, my study was a study of changing institutions, of the ways in which a simpler, smaller-scale society had been and was being affected by contact with large-scale, Western institutions and values. Thus Nyoro chiefs were what they were in the 1950s, and were faced with the problems they were faced with, because they were the focus of a conflict between traditional and Western norms of government. The settlement of disputes in the native courts (themselves largely a Western invention) involved an uneasy synthesis of traditional and Western procedures. Nyoro traditional ritual, especially the *mbandwa* spirit mediumship cult, had radically changed its form under the influence of missions and government, and had adapted itself in various ways to the new conditions (some of these ways are described in Beattie 1961c). With the advent of a cash economy and a growing individualism, domestic life and conjugal and kinship relations were something very different from what they may be supposed to have been in traditional times. As I said in the last chapter of *Bunyoro,* there is scarcely any aspect of Nyoro social and cultural life in which traditional and contemporary values are not, in some degree, at odds with one another, and the analysis of the complex reality that this entails is the central task of the fieldworker in a modern African society. It was certainly my main concern in Bunyoro.

These considerations, I think, provide an answer to the criticism, sometimes made, that social anthropologists are so obsessed by fieldwork for its own sake that it has assumed for them a kind of mystique, and has become a sort of indispensable *rite de passage* for the aspiring professional. Regardless of its practical utility or lack of it, such critics say, it is essentially a ritual that must be performed by the novice before he can become one of the elect.

I think it is sufficiently plain that this is not or at least need not be so. Certainly the experience of living with and getting to know well a quite unfamiliar culture and people is, for most anthropologists, uniquely interesting and stimulating, and despite its possible discomforts and even dangers it is easy to romanticize it. But this does not make the task itself any less important or necessary. Whether it is in some exotic tropical island, in central Africa or New Guinea, or in the next parish, the field is the social anthropologist's laboratory. If it be agreed that his main task is to attempt to understand another culture or other cultures, then it will, I think, be acknowledged that he cannot do this adequately solely at second hand. This is not to say that there is no place in the subject for "armchair anthropologists," who can take a broad comparative view of ethnographic material gathered by others: most certainly there is, and social anthropologists have been saying so for years. But the data have to be collected before they can be analysed and compared, and as I stressed at the beginning of this book, they have to be collected by trained scholars and not by amateurs. If social anthropologists do not do their own fieldwork, it is certain that nobody else will do it for them.

References*

BARNES, J. A., 1963, Some Ethical Problems in Modern Fieldwork. *British Journal of Sociology* 14, 3:118–134.

BEATTIE, J. H. M., 1959, Checks on the Abuse of Political Power in some African States: a Preliminary Framework for Analysis. *Sociologus* 9, 2:97–115.

———, 1964, *Other Cultures: Aims, Methods and Achievements in Social Anthropology.* London: Cohen and West.

EVANS-PRITCHARD, E. E., 1951, *Social Anthropology.* London: Cohen and West.

KABERRY, P., 1957, Malinowski's Contribution to Fieldwork Methods and the Writing of Ethnography. In *Man and Culture,* Raymond Firth (ed.). London: Routledge & Kegan Paul.

LIENHARDT, G., 1964, *Social Anthropology.* London: Oxford University Press (Home University Library of Modern Knowledge).

RICHARDS, A. I., 1939, The Development of Field Work Methods in Social Anthropology. In *The Study of Society: Methods and Problems,* F. Bartlett and others (eds.). London: Routledge & Kegan Paul.

——— (ed.), 1960, *East African Chiefs.* London: Faber and Faber.

ROSCOE, J., 1911, *The Baganda.* London: Macmillan.

———, 1923, *The Bakitara or Banyoro.* London: Cambridge University Press.

ROYAL ANTHROPOLOGICAL INSTITUTE OF GREAT BRITAIN AND IRELAND, 1951, *Notes and Queries on Anthropology* (6th edition). London: Routledge and Kegan Paul.

Publications on Bunyoro by the Author

1960   *Bunyoro: An African Kingdom.* New York: Holt, Rinehart and Winston, Inc.

---

* Publications on Bunyoro by the author are listed separately.

59

On the Nyoro State

1954   The *Kibanja* System of Land Tenure in Bunyoro, Uganda. *Journal of African Administration* 4, 1:18–28.
        A Further Note on the *Kibanja* System of Land Tenure in Bunyoro, Uganda. *Journal of African Administration* 4, 4:178–185.
1959   Rituals of Nyoro Kingship. *Africa* 29, 2:134–145.
1960a   The Nyoro. In *East African Chiefs,* Audrey Richards (ed.). London: Faber and Faber.
1961a   Democratization in Bunyoro. *Civilisations* 11, 1:8–20.
1964   Bunyoro: an African Feudality? *Journal of African History* 5, 1:25–36.

On the Nyoro Community

1957   Nyoro Kinship. *Africa* 27, 4:317–340.
        Informal Judicial Activity in Bunyoro. *Journal of African Administration* 9, 4:188–195.
1958   Nyoro Marriage and Affinity. *Africa* 28, 1:1–22.
        The Blood Pact in Bunyoro. *African Studies* 17, 4:198–203.
1960b   Homicide and Suicide in Bunyoro. In *African Homicide and Suicide,* P. Bohannan (ed.)., Princeton, N.J.: Princeton University Press.
        Bunyoro through the Looking Glass. *Journal of African Administration* 12, 2:85–94.
1964   The Story of Mariya and Yozefu: a Case Study from Bunyoro, Uganda. *Africa* 34, 2:105–115.
1965   Matiyo and his Two Wives: a Further Case Study from Bunyoro. *Africa* 35, 3:252–262.

On Nyoro Ritual

1957   Nyoro Personal Names. *Uganda Journal* 21, 1:99–106.
        Initiation into the Cwezi Spirit Possession Cult in Bunyoro. *African Studies* 16, 3:150–161.
1960c   The Nyoro Concept of *Mahano. African Studies* 19, 3:145–150.
1961b   Nyoro Mortuary Rites. *Uganda Journal* 25, 2:171–183.
1961c   Group Aspects of the Nyoro Spirit Mediumship Cult. *Rhodes-Livingstone Journal* 30:11–38.
1962   Twin Ceremonies in Bunyoro. *Journal of the Royal Anthropological Institute* 92, 1:1–12.
1963   Sorcery in Bunyoro. In *Witchcraft and Sorcery in East Africa,* J. Middleton and E. H. Winter (eds.). London: Routledge & Kegan Paul.

1963   A Note on the Connexion between Spirit Mediumship and Hunting in Bunyoro, with Special Reference to Possession by Animal Ghosts. *Man* 63 241:188–189.

1964   Divination in Bunyoro, Uganda. *Sociologus* 14, 1:44–62.
        The Ghost Cult in Bunyoro. *Ethnology* 3, 2:127–151.
        Rainmaking in Bunyoro. *Man* 64 179:140–141.